REFLECTIONS OF VALOUR

REFLECTIONS OF VALOUR

JAMES ELSENER

Ledger Publishing, Inc.

CONTENTS

© Copyright 2021

ISBN 978-1-949661-50-7

Published by Ledger Publishing Company

Chicago, Illinois

Publication services provided by Fort Raphael Publishing Co., Oak Park, IL (fortraphael.com)

Cover design by Touchstone Graphic Design

PRAISE FOR "REFLECTIONS OF VALOUR"

Had me hooked from page one...twists back in time through love, war, and devotion. A tender story with a raw edge.

Robert Goldsborough
Author – Nero Wolfe Mysteries

Reflections of Valour brings to life the experiences of a young Marine during the calm before the war when he meets his first love to his fate in 1967 Vietnam. The story takes him from a college sorority event to an artillery unit in Vietnam. What makes the book so readable is that it perfectly captures the idealism and innocence of the time and the reality of war. I was a Marine in that period. The book tells it exactly right.

William Donohue, President
Donohue-Meehan Publishing Co.

The Vietnam Veterans Memorial - The Wall, serves as a backdrop for the experiences of young lovers who must deal with the war of their generation. *Reflections of Valour* is a love story and a war story that reflects the decisions faced by men in uniform and their loved ones. The author has a distinct ability to describe the places and introduce his characters in well-written dialogue. The last sentence in the book is a totem for his style of writing and storytelling.

Russell Fee
Author – The Award-Winning Sherriff Matt Callahan Mystery Series

Those of us who lived through the early Vietnam War era as college students will never forget the confusion and conflict that clouded our lives and future. The war at home was just as intense as the war in Vietnam. *Reflections of Valour* is on target in catching the complete flavor of that time and its aftermath including the symbolism of The Wall and the devastating effects of Agent Orange. This is a book that's easy to recommend to my generation and money well spent.

Mike Conklin
Author – Transfer U.; and Goal Fever!

Dedicated to the Memory of
First Sergeant Donald G. Plavnick, USMC

Glossary of Military Jargon

2/9 – Two-Nine. Second Battalion, 9th Marine Regiment. 3rd Division.

3/8 – Third Battalion, 8th Marine Regiment, 2nd Division.

105-mm– The 105-millimeter howitzer was the standard artillery piece used by the Marines in Vietnam.

155mm – The 155-millimeter howitzer (self-propelled) had a range of about 9 miles.

782 gear – Standard-issue Marine combat gear, mainly the pack, poncho, utility shovel, ammunition belt and suspenders.

8" (inch) Howitzer (self-propelled) – The King of Battle. The largest artillery used by the Marines in Vietnam. Its shell weighed 203 pounds with an effective range of 12.5 miles. Maximum range is 20 miles.

ARVN – Army of the Republic of (South) Vietnam.

ASAP – As soon as possible.

Battalion – Approximately 1,200 to 1,300 Marines and sixty naval medical personnel, four rifle companies, one headquarters and supply company (H&S) that includes 81-millimeter mortars, communications, mess, medical and administrative personnel.

Battery – Artillery unit roughly equivalent in size to a rifle company. One battery was normally assigned to one infantry battalion.

B-Ration – Packaged unprepared food prepped in mess halls or field kitchens. The usual meals of an artillery battery on a firebase.

Bird or Chopper – A helicopter. The Marines primary ride was the CH-46.

Butter Bar – A second lieutenant, often new and inexperienced, so called because the rank is designated by a single gold bar.

Claymore – Fan-shaped antipersonnel land mind. It produced a fan-shaped pattern of fragments and was usually placed aboveground in front of a fighting hole or alongside a trail for an ambush.

CO – Commanding Officer

Corpsmen – Navy medical personnel assigned to the Marine units.

CP – Command Post

C-ration – Often called C-rats. Prepared food when fresh food was not available.

Charlie – Nickname used by Marines for Viet Cong troops.

Crotch – Slang for the United States Marine Corps.

DMZ – Demilitarized zone between the borders of North and South Vietnam.

DOD – United States Department of Defense.

EM – Enlisted Men's Club

Entrenching Tool – Called an E-tool. A small folding shovel about two feet long carried by all combat Marines. Designed to dig fighting holes.

FDC - Fire Direction Center. The part of a command post that controls and directs artillery fire.

Field(s) of Fire – Area that a weapon or group of weapons can cover effectively.

Firebase – A temporary artillery firing position.

Fire Mission – Artillery mission.

FO – Forward Observer. Calls for artillery fire missions.

Friendly Fire – Weapons fire coming from one's own side.

GI – Government issue. Refers to American military personnel.

Gooks – Derogatory term describing anyone of Asian origin.

Green Machine – The United States Marine Corps.

Grunts – Infantry.

Gung ho –Enthusiastic and committed.

Gunny – A company / battery gunnery sergeant (E-7). Serves as the unit's operations chief.

Green Berets – Members of the U.S. Army Special Forces. Their uniform headgear is a green beret.

HE – High explosive artillery round.

H&I – Harassment and Interdiction fire. Unobserved artillery missions fired at random intervals seeking to deny enemy freedom of movement and to destroy morale.

Hooch – The standard field tent that provided sleeping quarters for Marines in a firebase.

I-Corps – The northern most area of military operations in South Vietnam. Headquarters were in Danang.

KIA – Killed in Action.

Lifer – Someone who is making the military a career. "Lifer" was quite often a derogatory label. It implied that the lifer put career, military rules, and decorum above the welfare of the troops.

LP / OP - Listening Post/ Observation Post. Usually a team of two Marines placed outside the defenses at night with a radio. Their job was to listen for enemy movement and provide early warning.

LT – Nickname for lieutenant.

LZ – A landing zone for helicopters.

M-14 – Standard issue semi-automatic rifle used at the beginning of the Vietnam War. It could fire automatic if equipped with a selector switch. It was replaced in 1968 by the M-16.

Medevac – Medical evacuation by helicopter.

MOS – Military Occupational Specialty.

Mustang – An officer who is promoted from the enlisted ranks.

NCO – Non-commissioned officer (ranks E4-E9).

NVA – North Vietnamese Army, the regular army of the People's Republic of Vietnam (PAVN).

OP – Observation Post. Serves the same purpose as an LP (Listening Post).

Platoon – Three squads form a platoon. It was designated to have 43 Marines.

Pond – Slang for Pacific Ocean. Used as in the term "Across the Pond."

PRC 6 – Pronounced "Prick six." Handheld radio often referred to as a "walkie-talkie." Maximum range 1 mile. Used by listening posts, fire team and squad leaders working in close combat.

PRC 10 – Pronounced "Prick ten." Standard backpack radio used for platoon communications. Replaced in Vietnam by the PRC 25.

PRC 25 – Pronounced "Prick twenty-five," FM radio used by all Marine infantry units in Vietnam.

Round-eyes – Slang for American and European women, to be distinguished from Asian women who were derisively referred to as "slant eyes."

R&R – Rest and Recreation. Marines were given a five-day R&R once during their thirteen-month tour of duty in Vietnam. Popular destinations were Hong Kong, Taipei, Hawaii, Bangkok, Sydney.

S-3 – Battalion operations office.

Search and Destroy – Offensive military operations

Semper Fi – Short for Semper Fidelis, Latin for "always faithful," the Marine Corps motto.

SP – Self-propelled artillery mounted on a tank-like body that can be driven rather than towed.

TAOR – Tactical area of responsibility.

The Wall – Vietnam Veterans Memorial.

Tracers – Illuminated (green) bullets that allows a rifleman to track its path.

VC – Vietcong, the guerilla army based in South Vietnam and supplied by the North Vietnamese. Marines referred to them as VC or Charlie.

Wake-up – Last day "in country" before going home / or being discharged.

WIA – Wounded in action.

XO – Executive Officer – second in command.

"Don't cheer boys. The poor devils are dying."
Rear Admiral (USN) John Woodward Phillip
Spanish-American War – July 3, 1898
As he watched the burning of the Spanish cruiser Vizcaya

The First American to die in Vietnam was Lieutenant Colonel Peter Dewey (US Army), head of the OSS Mission, on September 26, 1945, when he was mistaken for a Frenchman. Prior to his death he filed a report that the U.S. *"...ought to clear out of Southeast Asia."*
Vietnam War Almanac by James Wilbanks

PROLOGUE

When Brenda saw his name on The Wall it was as if she had suddenly recalled an entire horror movie she had seen as a teenager. It was a memory long repressed that now almost instantly brought tears to her eyes and a churning of her stomach that comes with a feeling of panic.

It had been more than two decades since she had seen him, and many years had passed since she thought of him for anything more than a passing moment. As she saw his name etched on The Wall she felt as if she could reach out and touch his face. It was his smile that reflected off the polished black granite, not hers.

"Oh," she heard herself whisper involuntarily. Her fingers slowly traced the letters etched in The Wall. *John Briggs.* The names are grouped under the date of their death. His was February 8, 1967. She tried to think what she was doing that day, but instead she reflected on a day, 18 months before that in August 1965.

She was on a Trailways Bus on Highway 17 north of Myrtle Beach when he had first spoken with her. That was 23 years ago.

"Mom! Mom!" She became aware of a tugging at her arm. "Mom, c'mon down here. Dad found the name of a guy he was in college with."

Brenda now allowed herself to be pulled along the sidewalk by her son, no different than John Briggs had been pulled away from her years before. For these few moments she felt like a person living in two worlds.

"Honey. Here is a guy I knew my freshman year at Princeton," Jay said. "Bobby Hearn. He lived down the hall from me in the dorm. Big guy. Red hair. I think he was ROTC. I heard he had gone to Vietnam. This has got to be him. Robert L. Hearn. I don't remember his middle initial. But I'll bet that was him. Just about the right time he would have been over there. January 1970."

Jay's attention was on the name in front of him. He never looked at Brenda while he spoke. She took the opportunity to brush away a tear.

"Did you know him well, Dad?" Steven asked. "Was he a good friend of yours?"

"No. Not really Steven. I maybe talked to him a half dozen times. Seemed like a good guy."

"Wow." Steven, 11 years old, was obviously impressed that his father had come close enough to a war to know someone who had died in it.

This was supposed to have been a fun family vacation in Washington, D.C. Jay was the one who wanted to visit The Wall, the memorial to the dead of the Vietnam War. This was the war of Brenda and Jay's generation, which they preferred to forget. It was a war that hardly touched them or their families and friends. It was a war fought by a different economic class.

Jay had managed to stay out of the military by having college deferments and then the luck of a high draft lottery number. Most of their friends did the same. It was only an occasional acquaintance who had served. The Vietnam War was not one that intruded much on the lives of the upper economic classes.

"Why do you want to take the boys to something like that?" she asked him before leaving the hotel room. "It's something just best forgotten."

She saw no reason for telling Jay her real reason for not wanting to visit the most popular monument in the nation's capital. There were just these strong negative feelings she got whenever The Wall was mentioned.

"C'mon honey. They say it's really a moving experience. Everyone who comes to D.C. goes to see it."

"Yeah, Mom. We saw all the pictures of it at school. What's the big deal?" Eric was 14, her oldest. He was born during the years when the war was winding down.

She knew it was a losing battle but decided to play bitch to the end, a tactic she often utilized with the males in her family. They always out-voted Brenda on ballgames over concerts, war monuments over art galleries and hamburgers with fries over "dress for dinner."

"It's cold out there. Look at it. I don't want to stand out there and freeze looking at some monument."

Together the three males she loved more than anything in the world moaned in disgust and looked at her with eyes most often reserved for "sissies."

"Okay. Okay. I'll go. But you guys have to give in to me on occasion." This is how they always resolved these things. She knew if she protested enough, she would win her share of the decisions by appealing to the male guilt vote.

Coming to Washington for the Thanksgiving holidays had been Brenda's idea. She had spent four years at Mary Washington College in Fredericksburg, Virginia, 50 miles south, and had always loved coming into the city. She had been a political science major and dreamed of a career in government seeing herself in a major policy making role.

Instead, she had done all the traditional things expected of a young woman in those days. She graduated, moved home for a while and then to New York where she got a job with a book publishing company. She met Jay who was a student at Columbia Law. They got married during his second year. Eric was born two years later and Steven 3 years after Eric. Jay ended up working on Wall Street. They moved to suburban New Jersey and her career now consisted of serving as the volunteer president of the Fair Lawn Infant Welfare Society.

They had driven down on Friday morning having spent Thanksgiving Day with his parents. It was only a four-hour drive but one they had never made before as a family.

"Jay. The boys are getting older. We need to show them Washington. It's a short drive. If we can take them to Disney World, we certainly should be able to take them to something as important as Washington," she argued.

"I'll bet they like Disney World better," Jay had countered knowing it would get his wife to wrinkle up her nose and stick her tongue out. He felt she never aged when she did that. Cute as the day he met her...although she hated it when he called her "cute."

"No doubt. You probably like Disney World better too."

"There's no Space Mountain in D.C., is there?"

She ignored him.

The drive down had been completed under gray skies predicted by the weather service to continue throughout the weekend with a possibility of the first snow flurries of the year. It did not seem to affect anyone's spirits. They had checked into the hotel and the boys immediately changed into their swimming suits and headed for the indoor pool.

Brenda and Jay raided the mini bar. He had a craft beer which was imported and for which the hotel charged eight bucks. "I could buy a six-pack of this stuff in in Jersey for that much," he said.

"Honey. This is a nice hotel. Let's not worry about the prices. Let's just have an enjoyable time. Who cares what it costs?" She settled for a small bottle of Chardonnay. The price was the same as the beer. She noticed the price despite her lecture to Jay. It was not as if they couldn't afford it or had never stayed in 4-star hotels before. It is just something everyone notices when they are getting gouged.

They took off their shoes, laid on the bed and started paging through various tourist publications that were in the room.

"Where do you want to go first?" Jay asked.

"Let's just relax for a bit. Then we'll worry about where we are going later. Pick out a nice place for dinner first."

Jay stared at his wife, a smile beginning to creep into the corners of his mouth. "Honey." He emphasized the "e" turning it into a long mocking whine. Then he switched into a deep but artificial baritone imitating an old-time radio announcer. "We can relax and eat in New Jersey. We need to get out there and hit those monuments. These kids must develop an appreciation for the most powerful city on earth. We need to infuse in them the principles that guided our founding fathers. We will start with the National Archives. The Bill of Rights. Then we'll walk down Pennsylvania Avenue, the most famous avenue in the world. Well, next to Madison Avenue maybe. We'll see the FBI, the Capitol, the Library of Congress, PJ's adult book store and video arcade, the old post office..."

He got no further before she threw a pillow at him.

"I didn't get to finish," he protested.

"You're finished. Believe me."

* * * * * * * * * * * * * *

November 1988
Washington, DC

The first two days in Washington Brenda and her family were constantly on the go. Everyone was now tired and had seen enough. They were planning on heading back to New Jersey after hotel check out on Sunday. The boys wanted one more swim in the hotel pool. Jay said he would serve as the adult on duty.

Brenda told Jay she wanted to go back to a couple of local shops they had passed the previous day to pick up some Christmas gifts with a nation's capital theme.

"Okay honey. We'll meet you back here about 12:45. Check out is at 1," Jay said. "Let's hit it boys." They left in a hurry dressed in their swimming trunks with towels over their arms.

Seeing the image of his name on The Wall had hung heavy on her the past two days. She needed to go back and see it again. It being a quiet Sunday morning she found a cab waiting in line outside the hotel front door.

"The Vietnam Memorial please." It was a typical late November day, temperatures in the high 30's, overcast and gray. A few snow flurries promised winter was close.

The cabbie navigated the empty streets to The Wall in less than 10 minutes. She gave him a ten-dollar bill and told him to keep the change, a very generous tip on a six-dollar cab ride, but she did not want to get into a discussion of taxi rates. Like many tourists, Brenda never did understand the Washington zone rate system. The price did not show up on a meter like it did in New York. For visitors, you just had to trust that you were being charged the right amount or spend a few minutes trying to understand the zone map on the back of the driver's seat.

Like many D.C. cab drivers, he was a recent immigrant from Africa with an accent Brenda did not want to try interpreting.

It was about a quarter mile walk to The Wall. She felt winter in the air as she turned up her coat collar. She had unintentionally left her scarf, hat and gloves in the hotel room as she was in a hurry to leave. She would just have to hunch up her shoulders and tough it out.

There were only three other people at the memorial. One middle aged woman was busy tracing a name. An older couple was standing arm in arm in silence.

The Wall has an impact on visitors. The names of more than 57,000 dead in a war without a clear purpose or a victory speaks volumes. Touching the name of a loved one provides some connection to the past and an overwhelming feeling of sadness. Anyone who was of an age during that period will carry those memories to their own graves.

Brenda found panel 15-E which listed the deaths in February 1967. John Briggs was near the top. She took a couple of deep breaths, stepped up and touched his name with her fingertips, pushing harder until her fingers lost their color. She moved her fingers back and forth over his name. Her eyes were wet.

How her life would have been different, not that it would be better. Just different. She would never regret her marriage to Jay and being a mother to her boys. That wasn't the issue. It was just a sadness for a love that she had over two decades before that she had never totally forgotten. It was a first love that ended without a final chapter.

Here was a moment when she was with John again wanting to hold him and tell him things would be alright. They would have a life together.

Instead, all she had was his name etched in stone on her fingertips and a memory of his voice telling her he loved her. They had their dreams together. She thought of them being a family.

As she removed her hand, she felt like she had when he left for Vietnam. For some reason she could not understand, she felt responsible for his name being on The Wall.

There was a bench a few feet away. She sat down not feeling the cold so much but instead a deep sense of sadness and regret. She looked at the rest of The Wall which seemed to stretch forever. The stories of so many were told in those names on black granite.

When she saw others tracing names, she wondered why someone would want to do that. But now as she thought about leaving the memorial and the memories of him, she decided to do the same. She carried a notebook in her purse. She tore out a piece of paper and placed it against his name. She lightly traced it with her pencil as she had seen others do. This did give Brenda something to take with her. It was a piece of Johnny Briggs.

It was time to head back to the hotel. She walked slowly towards the Washington Monument a mile away. She caught a cab and had the driver drop her about six blocks from the hotel. Her heart and her head were not into shopping, but she needed to come back with a few gifts. She did not want to have to lie or explain how she had spent the morning.

She found a jigsaw puzzle of the Lincoln Memorial that the boys would enjoy, and a red, white, and blue winter scarf and socks for Jay. He would make some funny remark about the patriotic theme, but she knew he would enjoy wearing them.

It was 12:35 on the lobby clock when she got back to the hotel, 10 minutes before Jay's departure deadline. When she got to the room the boys were on the bed watching TV. They totally ignored their mother's arrival. Jay was putting the last touches on packing.

"So how did you do," he asked. He had just glanced briefly at her when she walked in but kept fiddling with the suitcases and trying to make everything fit.

"Yeah. Fine. I got a couple things," she said holding up her bag. "But they are for Christmas. So, no peeking. It was cold out there. I limited my wandering spirits to go from store to store. Plus, everything is so darn expensive. So, I shopped smart."

She was not sure that Jay even heard her as he began to rally the boys.

"Giddy up guys. It's roundup time. We're burning daylight. Do a look around to make sure you have everything and take a final pee check. No stopping until we hit Jersey."

Brenda knew that message was meant for her too. The entire family was tired. It was a quiet car ride home, which was okay with her. Jay did the driving while she put her head back, closed her eyes and locked her thoughts away.

PART I

Panel 1-E, Line 1, Vietnam Veterans Memorial
U.S. Army Major Dale R. Buis, 37, Pender, Nebraska,
died July 8, 1959,
from an explosive device in Bien Hoa Province, South Vietnam.

CHAPTER 1

August 1965
Myrtle Beach, South Carolina

Vietnam Timeline: In Operation Starlite, some 5,500 U.S. Marines strike against the Vietcong in the first major ground offensive by U.S. forces in Vietnam.

Brenda Kiley was heading home to New Jersey before she began her senior year of college. Despite her father's disapproval she had spent her summer as a waitress in a Myrtle Beach seafood restaurant and shared an apartment with three other girls. They worked for low wages and tips with an opportunity to spend time on the beach.

It was a Sunday morning. Hot and humid like it can be in the south during late August. She faced a 9-hour bus trip home to Ardmore, a toney Philadelphia suburb, but it was the way she wanted to do it. Her father had offered to send her a plane ticket, but this was part of showing independence. Having made her own money this summer and paying her own expenses, she had become aware of the cost of living. Brenda's father was a big bucks Philadelphia attorney. He paid her college expenses and offered her a summer job in his law firm. But she took the job in Myrtle Beach to show him that she could support herself.

Brenda quit her job three days before but stayed around the weekend to party with friends and get the last few days on the beach. Most of the kids followed the same routine as they began packing up and heading back to reality.

The 9 a.m. bus on Sunday morning was not the most popular in the bible belt where church services took precedence. Brenda was one of only five passengers who boarded. There were two young men about her age who she noted were attractive but disheveled looking as if they had slept on the beach the night before, not all that uncommon in Myrtle Beach. Their haircuts gave them away as military.

There was also an older black couple onboard who Brenda knew would be getting off at some rural stop up the road.

Brenda was feeling good. Despite all the summer ending parties she had gone to bed relatively early having been up late Friday night. She knew the bus ride would be long and she did not want to endure it being tired and cranky.

As the bus pulled out of the station, she kept her eyes out the window, saying goodbye to the first summer on her own. Being at school was not like being away or independent. She lived in a dormitory where you just showed up for meals.

She occasionally glanced at the two guys in the seats across the aisle. They talked to one another sparingly, spending more time with their heads back and eyes closed. She sensed that they had noticed her. She had caught their quick glances.

The bus stopped twice within the next half hour as it crossed the North Carolina border. The elderly black couple got off at a rural road crossing while a large, middle aged black woman carrying several bags got on. The bus driver greeted her by name as she shuffled to a seat near the back.

"Where you headed?"

Brenda was surprised by the question then realized it had been asked of her by one of the guys across the aisle. He was looking at her.

"Huh? Oh. I'm sorry. Did you say something to me?" She realized he couldn't have been talking to anyone else and felt a bit flustered.

"Yeah. I was. Just wondering where you were headed?" Brenda noted that he needed a shave. His dark brown hair needed combing. His shirt was wrinkled. She saw the eagle, globe and anchor tattoo on his well-muscled forearm. His smile was warm and inviting and despite his physical appearance she felt attracted to him. She knew there had to be a good reason he looked the way he did. His opening line wasn't original, but it would do.

"Ardmore, Pennsylvania. It's a suburb of Philadelphia. I'm going home to start school." She smiled back at him. "How about you?"

"We're headed back to Camp Lejeune. We just came down for the night and ended up having to sleep on the beach." He nodded at his buddy who was unconscious.

"What were you doing down here," he asked.

"I just spent the summer working. A lot of college kids do that. Camp Lejeune. That's Army, right?"

"Army? No way." He answered louder than she thought was necessary, but it was obvious he considered that comment an insult, or at least uninformed.

"Marines. All marine bases are camps. The army calls their bases forts."

"Oh. I didn't know that. I'm sorry."

"Where's school?"

"I go to Mary Washington College in Fredericksburg, Virginia. It's a woman's college. Liberal arts. It's named after George Washington's mother."

"Guess they don't have a football team," he commented.

"Obviously," she answered sharply and looked out the window feeling a bit stung by his smart aleck manner. She was sensitive about her choice of schools, seeing how it was really her father who insisted that she go there.

Mary Washington had a reputation as a suitcase college where the students headed each weekend for schools like the University of Virginia or to Georgetown and its lineup of nearby singles bars. The girls that stayed on campus each weekend were those with visiting boyfriends or no interest in acquiring any.

"What are you doing down here," he asked. Obviously, he had not paid attention to her original answer.

"Like I said, I've been working here for the summer. Waitressing." She felt good about her answer. It made her sound like a normal working stiff rather than a pampered girl's school preppie. This was what she had been trying to achieve this summer, to become a regular person.

"Yeah. Do a lot of partying, I'll bet."

"It's been fun." She glanced out the window again not sure if she wanted to continue the discussion. He was certainly different from the boys she knew, even those at Myrtle Beach who now were heading back to places like Clemson, George Tech, Duke and other academic kingdoms of the south.

"My buddy here is sort of out of it." He flipped his head towards the sleeping body in the seat beside him. "Mind if I join you?"

She knew he was hitting on her, but on a bus she was not overly concerned. If he got bothersome, she could always ask the driver to help her out. She trusted her instincts. Eventually, he had to get off the bus before her stop. She thought it was a good way to kill time on an otherwise boring trip through Tidewater. And, he was certainly different than her father would think appropriate. She found that many personal decisions were based upon choosing the opposite of what she thought her father would think best.

"Well, okay. Sure." She picked up her paperback book from the seat next to her, a clear message that he could join her. She momentarily felt embarrassed that she was allowing herself to be picked up on a Trailways Bus. She felt for sure that the bus driver was being judgmental while watching through his rearview mirror.

"My name is John Briggs. They call me Briggsy."

"Brenda Kiley." She was not sure if she should offer to shake hands. She found that introducing herself was always awkward. For some reason she thought her name did not sound right.

"Glad to meet you Brenda. So, tell me about Mary Washington College. All girls, huh? Sounds like a place I ought to be familiar with."

His lame attempt at humor put Brenda on the defensive. She answered with an edge in her voice that told him he was treading on sensitive ground.

"Academically we are one of the top colleges on the east coast."

"Oh. I'm sure. Didn't mean anything by that. I'm just talking. So. Myrtle Beach. A good place to spend the summer?"

"Yes. I had a good time. It's hard to head back to school." Deep down she knew that she had enjoyed the summer due as much to her father disliking her decision to work there as to the college kids' fun and games.

"Yeah. I'll bet. Maybe I'll do something like that when I get out of the Marine Corps."

"When will that be?"

"Next July. 330 and a wakeup."

"Pardon me?"

"That's just Marine lingo for counting the days until I get out. You know, 330 days and when I wake up on the morning of day 331, they give me my discharge papers and that's it. Adios. I gave 'em four years. They gave me 3 slops and a flop."

He could tell she did not pick up on that either. "You know. Three meals each day and a place to sleep. Three slops and a flop."

"Oh. Okay." She wasn't sure if this was going well or not. She thought he was attractive enough. His smile particularly seemed to draw her in. His eyes slightly crinkled at the corners, his cheeks puffed, and he showed lots of teeth. Very uninhibited and self-confident. A bit on the cocky side. She thought his lips looked very kissable. But she was still uneasy. It was clear they were communicating on different wavelengths. She was not sure how to get out of this situation, or if she wanted to. She noticed that he included the words "you know," in most of his sentences, a phrase that was frowned upon in her social circle as an affliction of the uneducated.

Brenda flattened herself against the window, arms crossed, turning slightly to face him. This put distance between them but also allowed her to look at him without turning her head. Briggs slouched in the aisle seat.

He told her that he and his buddy, whose name was just "Mitchell," or "Mitch for short," had hitchhiked down to the resort beach town the day before. After drinking too much in the boardwalk bars, they had spent the night sleeping on the beach. This came as no surprise to her.

"We probably look pretty groady, don't we?"

She laughed and agreed with him. Privately she thought he was cute, a description he would probably not like to hear. It would not fit with his warrior self-image.

Briggs was wearing a red plaid, short-sleeved cotton shirt with a button-down collar that showed off his tanned and muscular arms. She focused on his left forearm, a tattoo of the Marine Corps emblem, an anchor, globe and eagle underlined by the words "Semper Fi." She had never known anyone with a tattoo before.

"What's Semper Fi mean?"

"Always faithful. That's the Marine motto. Probably the dumbest thing I've ever done."

"What?" She wasn't sure what he was talking about.

"You know. The tattoo. Not a smart thing to do. I thought my folks would have a conniption fit when they saw it."

"Why did you do it."

"I was with some of my buddies after we got out of boot camp. I was at radio school. MCRD San Diego. That stands for Marine Corps Recruit Depot. With all the Navy in town there is a tattoo parlor on every corner. We got a little drunk and it just seemed like a gung-ho type of thing to do. We all got 'em. I liked it for a while. Then I got tired of looking at it. My arm never looks clean. But it is what it is. I will have it for the for the rest of my life. I guess there are worst things I could have done."

Brenda was not used to young men admitting their mistakes. The boys she knew never seemed to admit being wrong about anything. As she and Briggs talked, she found herself relaxing, enjoying the conversation. At first, he asked all the questions. It was the usual get acquainted, small talk conversation starters. She told him she had just turned 21 and was starting her senior year, majoring in political science and had been elected pledge chairman of her sorority.

"What's that? Kind of like a recruiting sergeant, I guess, huh?" Though she could not exactly relate to his analogy, she figured it was probably close enough.

"I guess so. I never thought of it quite that way before." She returned his smile and his questions.

Briggs was also 21, soon to turn 22. He had been in the Marines just over three years. He was a corporal. He seemed proud of being a squad leader, whatever that was. She was not exactly sure where a corporal fit in the military hierarchy.

He was from Battle Creek, Michigan. His parents both worked for Kellogg's, the cereal company. His father was a foreman in one of the processing plants. His mother was a bookkeeper. After graduating from Battle Creek Central High School, he had attended the local community college –Kellogg CC, but was tired of school and decided to enlist.

"Better than working for Kellogg's," he told her. "I can't stand the sight of corn flakes."

"It always seemed to me that all the kid's TV shows that I watched were sponsored by Kellogg's," Brenda said. "I was always using my allowance to buy some gadget like a Sky King Decoder Ring. You always had to send your money to Battle Creek, Michigan. I never met anyone before from Battle Creek."

"Yeah. If it wasn't for Kellogg's nobody would've ever heard of it."

She enjoyed his sense of humor and was disappointed when the bus pulled into the station in Jacksonville, North Carolina, gateway to the sprawling Camp Lejeune Marine Base. The time had gone too fast. She was not sure how to say goodbye, wishing he would be staying on the bus.

"You know, we get up to D.C. every so often on liberty. We go right through Fredericksburg. Well sort of. On I-95. Maybe I can stop and see you one of these times. Would that be okay? I promise I'll look better next time. I shine up like a new penny."

"Sure. That would be fun." Brenda thought she sounded trite but didn't know how else to answer him. She gave him her school address.

She was pleased that he wanted to see her again, but she thought she would never seem him again. It seemed like all talk.

CHAPTER 2

September 1965
Fredericksburg, Virginia

"Brenda? Is Brenda Kiley there?"

The distorted, tinny voice scrambled through the dormitory inter-com system. It sounded as if the speaker was in the bathroom. Brenda had been in her walk-in closet trying to decide which blouse to pack for the trip to Charlottesville. It was Saturday morning. Brenda and three friends were going for the night to attend a party at a UVA sister soror-ity.

She pushed the button allowing her to talk and put her lips close to the speaker box on the wall. "This is Brenda."

"You have a visitor at the front desk."

Brenda was not expecting anyone. She had no idea who her visitor might be. She shrugged her shoulders at Mary Thorsen, her roommate who was sitting in their one easy chair that was stuffed into the small but efficient dormitory room.

"Uh...who is it? I'm getting ready to leave for the weekend."

"Just a minute," the operator said. Brenda usually recognized the voice of the duty receptionist. This one was unfamiliar. She tried to pic-ture who it was but came up blank.

"It's a...Mister Briggs."

Brenda was baffled. She again shrugged her shoulders at Mary.

The voice came through the box again. "He says his name is Corporal John Briggs. United States Marine Corps." The receptionist seemed to be amused at this last piece of information.

"Uh. Okay. I'll be right down." She released the button, looked at Mary and said, "Omigod! That's the Marine I met this summer on the bus coming home from Myrtle Beach. What's he doing here? What am I going to do?"

"A Marine?" Mary questioned. "You never mentioned him to me before. Aren't we just a little slut? Getting picked up on a bus by a Marine. Fleet was in or what?" She was amused by the situation.

"Oh. Well, he's cute. But what's he doing here? He's supposed to be someplace in North Carolina."

"Want me to go down and get rid of him? I could say you just came down with a severe case of the bubonic plague."

"No!" Brenda shouted at Mary. "No. No. I'll go talk to him. I'm just surprised is all."

Brenda quickly pulled on a sweater, teased her hair and checked her makeup. "Jeez. This is a hell of a time for him to come by. When are we leaving?"

"About 25 minutes. Sharon is going to pick us up out front."

"Okay. I'll be there. Here's my bag. Bring it down for me please. Oh Christ. What am I going to say to this guy?" She mumbled to herself as she hurried out the door. Her room was on the third floor. It took her about two minutes to traverse the center stairway and reach the well-appointed lobby, a very proper reception room for a southern women's college furnished with faux colonial style furniture where the residents could properly entertain their guests in full view of the staff.

She saw him standing with hands in his pockets, his back to her, looking out one of the huge floor to ceiling windows that dominated the room. He was framed by the natural sunlight that made the reception area bright and warm. The windows offered a colorful view of the green, rolling campus dotted with giant black oak trees that framed the red brick and white trimmed buildings.

"John?" she said to his back. She was uncertain what her reaction would be. She couldn't exactly remember what he looked like, having pretty much forgotten him since returning to school a month ago. In fact, she wasn't even sure she was talking to the right person but not seeing any other men in the room she assumed it had to be him.

He turned around quickly pulling his hands out of his pockets. He smiled and looked her up and down. "Hi. Surprise! I hope you remember me."

"Of course, I do. Nice to see you again. I'm just a bit shocked, I guess."

She realized he was more nervous than she was. That made her feel more comfortable. He was better looking than she remembered. All she had in her mind was this scruffy looking guy who had spent the previous night sleeping on a beach and looked like it. Now he was clean shaven, his hair combed, wearing a blue-knit short sleeved golf shirt which showed off his well-tanned and muscular arms and neck. And, his tattoo, of course.

"I have to admit I'm surprised. I really didn't think I would see you again."

"Me neither. But, hell, I was going by Fredericksburg on I-95 and saw the sign for your college and thought why not? I'm headed to D.C. to meet up with a couple of buddies who are now stationed at Quantico. So, this is where you live, huh?" He looked around the room. "Nice. It's a lot better than the barracks. That's for sure."

Brenda could feel the awkwardness of the moment...for both of them.

"Why don't we sit down?" She gestured to a nearby couch. "John, I have to be honest with you. I was just getting ready to leave for Charlottesville with some of my friends. We're headed to UVA for the weekend. I've only got a few minutes I can talk."

Brenda glanced towards the reception desk where she saw Mary catching furtive glances of her and John. Mary sported a grin like a cat catching a mouse.

"Oh. Yeah. Well I understand, you know. I just drop in like this. It's not exactly the best thing. I'm glad I found you anyways. How's school going?"

"Fine. How long are you going to be in D.C?"

"Oh, just overnight. I bought a car since I last saw you. I got a little raise in pay when I hit three years in the Corps, plus the promotion to Corporal. So, I'm more mobile now. My buddies know all the good places in D.C."

"I'm sure you'll have a good time. Will you be coming back this way?" She began to wish she weren't going any place. He had a sweet way about him that she recalled from their meeting on the bus.

"Well, tomorrow, of course. I'll be heading back down this way. Camp Lejeune is five hours away. I'm not sure when I'll be back up this way again. Will you be back by tomorrow afternoon? Maybe I could stop by and we could get something to eat."

Brenda knew if she said "no" he probably would never come back and that would be the end of him. She didn't think she wanted that to happen. "I could be here about 3 p.m. or so. Would that be okay?"

"Yeah. Sure. Fifteen hundred hours." He paused. "That's 3 p.m. civilian time. I'll still be able to get back to base before midnight. It's a date."

Their goodbye was a bit awkward. No handshake. No hug. Just a quick "I'll see you tomorrow." Out the door he went.

On the trip to Charlottesville she filled her friends in on her meeting with John Briggs. Mary agreed that he was good looking but commented: "Brenda. The tattoo. Really? That just doesn't go over well at Mary Washington College."

"Yeah. I know. He's different. But, it's not like I'm marrying the guy. I'm just having dinner with him." She tried to put him out of her mind during the 90-minute trip to UVA, the sorority party that evening and the overnight. She had talked with a few guys during the party but no one who interested her much. Her mind kept drifting back to John Briggs. She was intrigued. She wasn't sure if it was a bad thing or a good thing that they were living in much different environments. She had never spent time with anyone in the military before.

Brenda decided she would wait in the lobby for him rather than making him go through the check-in at the front desk. He showed up promptly at 1500 hours, as he would describe it. She hated the awkward first date syndrome and could sense his nervousness.

Briggs' car was a dark blue 1965 Volkswagen bug that he had bought while on leave back in Michigan a month before.

She directed him to a restaurant about three miles from campus, called the Krystal Kitchen. There were a couple families with small children finishing up their Sunday afternoon late lunch – early dinner. It looked like the sort of place that also catered to senior citizens. Otherwise, it was empty. They got a booth by the big window at the front and engaged in small talk about their respective weekends.

"So, what are you going to do when you get out of the Marine Corps," she asked.

"I haven't figured that out yet. All our enlistments got extended 4 months. That's for the Vietnam build up. The Marine Corps needs to go from 190,000 troops to 250,000. So, they're making us stay in longer. There is even some talk about drafting people. The Marines don't draft. You volunteer.

"I was supposed to get out next July, but that's not going to happen. It looks like I will be in at least until November next year."

"So, will you have to go to Vietnam?"

"I guess that's a possibility. By the time they send me I might be a bit short. But I guess they could send me anyways."

"What do you mean, you're short?"

"Marines tour of duty in Vietnam is 13 months. Army is a year. Not sure why but it is what it is. By the time I get orders, go to Pendleton for training, and then they send me over, I might have less than 13 months to serve. Even with the extension. That's what short means. I would have to volunteer to extend my enlistment even more."

"You wouldn't do that, would you?"

He paused. "No one really wants to go to war. But you do train for this. It's what I've been doing for three plus years. They could use me over there. It sounds like a goofy thing to say, but when you join the Marines, or Army or any branch of service, you do it knowing you are getting ready for war."

Brenda had never had a discussion like this before. All the young men she knew were more concerned with their draft deferments and other ways of avoiding military service.

The topics of conversation drifted to their lives back home in Ardmore for her and Battle Creek for him. High school activities weren't too far in their rear-view mirrors so they each shared stories about that period of their lives, friends, and family. It was the usual first date getting-to-know-you conversation.

Briggs looked at his watch. They had been in the restaurant for over two hours. Talk had been easy. The first date jitters had gone away long before.

"I think they're going to kick us out of here before long and I guess I better be hitting the road. Hope you don't mind."

"No. I understand. This has been fun."

He pulled up in front of Brenda's dorm and walked her to the door. To kiss or not to kiss. That was the question running through both their minds as they said goodbye. It just seemed a very natural thing as they shared a quick kiss on the lips.

CHAPTER 3

September 1965
Camp Lejeune, North Carolina

Marine Corps Base Camp Lejeune is 246 square miles or 11,000 acres, however you want to measure it, of piney forests, sandy beaches and a good hunk of salt swamp, bordering the Atlantic Ocean and both banks of the New River tidal estuary.

Every Marine who has spent any time in one of Lejeune's training areas, has memories of dealing with chiggers, the base's signature insect. There is no escaping this mite that lives in forests and grasslands and causes severe itching.

The base is the economic engine of Onslow County, North Carolina, located in the coastal plain 120 miles southeast of Raleigh, the state capitol. It's blessed with warm days, cool nights, and ocean breezes.

Throughout the first half of the 20th century local citizens made their living in agriculture and the maritime industry. Lumber and tobacco were the main crops. Its rural nature began to change dramatically in 1941 with the creation of Camp Lejeune, named in honor of the 13th Commandant of the Marine Corps, "the Marine's Marine," General John A. Lejeune.

More than 40,000 Marines, families and civilian workforce comprise the Lejeune community.

If available to developers, Camp Lejeune's 14 miles of coastal beaches would be worth millions of dollars for vacation homes and seaside villas. Instead, the beach is used for amphibious assault training.

This is where Marines are taught to climb over the side of a transport ship on wobbly rope ladders, ride a bouncing landing craft two miles to shore and then trudge across a beach carrying 50 pounds of combat equipment hopefully without getting shot or blown up.

The deep-water ports of Morehead City to the north and Wilmington to the south allow for fast deployments. In addition, the giant U.S. Naval Base at Norfolk is just under four hours away.

Camp Lejeune is home to the 2nd Marine Division consisting of three infantry regiments – the 2nd Marines, the 6th Marines and the 8th Marines, and one artillery regiment – the 10th Marines. The 2nd Marine Division earned renown in World War II, distinguishing itself at Guadalcanal, Tarawa, Saipan, Tinian, and Okinawa.

Division headquarters are in Julian C. Smith Hall, a stately, collegiate looking brick building, five miles down Holcombe Boulevard from the base main gate and hard up against the shore of New River. The regimental barracks, all built during the 40s and 50s stretch in both directions. The 8th and 10th Marines occupy the buildings to the east while the 2nd and 6th Marines are to the west.

A Marine regiment consists of three battalions each of 1,000 men when fully staffed, which is rare. Each battalion is comprised of four rifle companies and one Headquarters & Service Company - administration, special weapons and communications.

Two-story barracks buildings were built in the shape of an H, each housing a company of about 150 men. Main squad bays on each floor accommodate 40 Marines in two-person bunk beds. Each Marine has a wall locker, and a footlocker that fits under the lower bunk. Boot camp teaches Marines how to keep all their worldly belongings in these confined spaces.

All the bunks and lockers are painted forest green. The walls a lighter shade of green. There is no air conditioning but surprisingly, 40 men living in the same room can agree on how much fresh air to allow through the windows each day.

The junior NCO quarters, for corporals and sergeants, are at the end of each squad bay and separated from the other troops by a line of wall lockers which provide some privacy. The NCOs sleep in single racks. That is their earned benefit.

Staff Sergeants and above, who do not live off base, rate one of the single occupancy rooms in the middle of each building across the hall from the head and showers.

Company headquarters are located on the first floor. A company rates a captain as its commanding officer – the CO, with a first lieutenant as the executive officer - the XO.

There is one-coin operated laundry, one barber shop and a small post exchange providing essentials only, serving each regiment.

The main post exchange, where a Marine and his family can purchase everything from shaving cream to cowboy hats to home appliances and groceries is located almost a mile away. A bowling alley is adjacent to the exchange.

The Main Side movie theater shows first run films and an occasional live performance. Other base theaters show a steady diet of Elvis Presley and beach bingo movies featuring hot looking women, music and fistfights. Marines love young Disney star Annette Funicello.

Privates, PFCs and lance corporals have their own enlisted man's (EM) clubs, known as the slop chute, featuring Falstaff and Carling Black Label beer for twenty-five cents a can. Food service consists of hot dogs baked under a heat lamp, chips, fries and candy bars. Entertainment is a juke box.

Corporals and sergeants drink among themselves at the NCO Club which has a full bar and serves sizzling T-Bone steaks for five dollars.

Officers and Senior NCOs do their drinking and socializing in their own upscale clubs. Making the CO's Friday night happy hour was required for young officers who want to make a successful career.

Stadiums for baseball and football, a field house and a guest hotel complete the Main Side complex.

Each notable building, structure and street is named after a famous dead Marine or a great battle. Cars drive on Holcombe Boulevard, Butler Road and Bougainville Street. Marine families live in Tarawa Terrace. Baseball is played at Agganis Field. Football at Liversedge Stadium.

There were travel sports teams in baseball, football and basketball representing the base and the Marine Corps. This is a hangover from earlier wars when professional athletes interrupted their careers to serve in the military. The players are treated like professionals, excused from other military activities to play games. The justification was that it was good for recruitment and public relations.

Camp Lejeune's satellite bases include the rifle range, Onslow Beach, the Infantry Training Center at Camp Geiger, the New River Air Station, Montford Point and Brown's Island, a salt swamp that serves as a practice bombing range for jets from the nearby Cherry Point Marine Corps Air Station.

All those facilities are spartan compared to Main Side. Everything is at least a half hour away. Bus service is provided hourly during daylight hours. Main Side to the rifle range, with several intermediate stops, 35 miles away, takes over an hour.

All Marines, cooks and clerks included, are considered riflemen. Every Marine is required to requalify annually at the range. That means a week spent in the farthest outpost of the base, where the amenities are few, the chow is bad, and the lines are long. Many of the personnel on mess hall duty or other administrative slots were sent there as punishment for disciplinary infractions. Nobody is happy to be at the range.

Special training schools and trailers for enlisted married housing are located at Montford Point. During World War II Montford Point was the basic training center for black Marines who served in segregated units. Railroad tracks divided the white residents from the training facility. Black recruits were not allowed to enter the main base unless accompanied by a white Marine.

At the beginning of the war, all drill instructors and training officers were white. As they got transferred overseas, they were replaced by black drill instructors.

In 1948 President Truman signed the order to desegregate the military but it did not happen overnight, particularly in the Marine Corps. The Montford Point boot camp was not deactivated until a year later and full integration took most of the next decade.

Just outside the base lies the city of Jacksonville known affectionately by the Marines as J'Ville. It was founded in 1842 and named in honor of former U.S. President Andrew Jackson. As Camp Lejeune evolved into a major military installation, Jacksonville took on the familiar profile of most towns located adjacent to a military base. The primary industry is focused on separating young Marines from their paychecks. The business community is dominated by bars, tattoo parlors, billiard halls, cheap motels, trailer parks, used car lots and pawn shops beginning just outside the main gate and running for seven miles along Lejeune Boulevard to downtown Jacksonville.

Neighborhoods near the base consist of ticky tacky little houses affordably priced for lifer sergeants and their families, to rent on short term leases.

This being part of the bible belt, the military and local police keep a sharp eye on vice activities, so prostitution is kept to a minimum. It was rumored that a Marine could find that type of entertainment in Wilmington, 50 miles to the south.

Even though Lejeune is a major military destination, it's not an easy place to get to using public transportation. The closest commercial airline service is provided by Piedmont Airlines out of New Bern 50 miles to the north. There are only two destinations – Washington, D.C. or Atlanta, Georgia, and being a small airport, service is often disrupted by inclement weather.

Downtown Jacksonville is segregated, not by law but by southern tradition. This is the Jim Crow South. A railroad track separates white Jacksonville from black Jacksonville. The bus station is located on the white side meaning that blacks must walk quickly through downtown to get to their side of the tracks.

The drinking age in North Carolina is 18 for beer. The age to buy hard liquor is 21 and it can only be purchased at a state licensed ABC (Alcohol Beverage Control) store. Most Marines settle for beer which is cheaper.

Jazzland and Birdland are the primary music bars in white Jacksonville. A typical Friday night consists of a group of young Marines disembarking at the bus station, a quick walk to Dewey's Restaurant where they order burgers and steaks and the first beer of the night.

Then they mosey across the street to Jazzland where they can sit for 3 hours nursing pitchers of beer and listening to music. The house band is Paul Peek and the Peekaboos. Paul Peek was a minor celebrity, being an early rockabilly pioneer who was a guitar player with Gene Vincent and the Blue Caps. Peek was one of the first rock stars to appear in a movie *"The Girl Can't Help It." (1956)*. It was always a mystery as to how his career could have dropped so low that he had a regular gig in Jacksonville.

The Peekaboos featured two female singers – Carol Lee, a buxom blond whose primary talent seemed to be in wearing low cut dresses and chiming in occasionally by shaking a tambourine; and Martha Brown, a few years older but still considered hot was a talented singer. The rest of the group comprised a drummer, a bass player and a rhythm guitar. Peek, of course, played the lead guitar and did most of the singing with one or both women.

Once a Marine and his buddies have a load on, they stagger out of the bar, head for the bus station and the ride back to base. The local bus company kept a few beat-up old buses for the evening trips to Camp Lejeune knowing that at least one or two of their passengers would get sick or abuse the bus in some other way. The bus was affectionately referred to as the "Vomit Comet."

CHAPTER 4

September 1965
Camp Lejeune, North Carolina

It was Motor Pool Monday for the Comm Platoon of H&S Company, Third Battalion, Eighth Marines. That meant a boring day of maintenance, cleaning and checking out the equipment of the eight radio jeeps assigned to the platoon.

Camp Lejeune was like a suitcase college on weekends. Friday afternoon hundreds of Marines would gather at the parking lot near the athletic fields known as The Circle to hitch rides with other Marines who had wheels and were anxious to share the gas expense for destinations up and down the east coast.

Many of them didn't return to base until the early morning hours on Monday, just making it back to the barracks before 5:30 a.m. reveille. Those who stayed on base spent too much time drinking in the bars in Jacksonville or at the EM and NCO clubs. An easy day of jeep maintenance was preferable to a day in the field training for war.

"Corporal Briggs. Take Newcombe, Fisher, Golubski and Weinman. You've got the four vehicles at the end of the line. Make sure to report any mechanical issues to the motor pool sergeant. Open all the radio cases and get in there with the brushes and clean them out. Give the jeeps a road test. Ten minutes is enough. I don't want any joy riding around the base. Inspection afterwards."

Staff Sergeant Ernie Lincoln was a by-the-book NCO with fourteen years in the Corps. He was tough but fair and respected by the troops, both black and white. An African American, he had enlisted during the Korean War when the Marine Corps was still coming to grips with integration. It was not a good time for blacks who were not easily accepted by the almost all white officer corps, many of them southerners, or the other enlisted men who resented any promotion earned by black Marines.

Lincoln wore a Silver Star earned during his service at the "frozen" Chosin Reservoir, the most famous Marine battle of the Korean Conflict. A Silver Star meant automatic respect of officers and troops. He never talked about it unless asked a direct question. He didn't need to. Everyone knew what it stood for.

"Any questions?" He waited briefly for a response, not expecting any. "Alright move out. I'll circle around before noon to inspect your work. Nobody cuts out for chow until I release you."

Lincoln went on with other assignments while Briggs gathered his work party. Now that he was an NCO he wasn't expected to join in the actual effort of cleaning and shining and buffing, but he did anyway. When he first joined the platoon, he was a private first class (PFC). He had made lance corporal after a year and then got the promotion to corporal six months later. He hadn't yet thought of himself as a boss supervising the work of others. He was still used to pitching in with the troops.

Newcombe and Fisher had been PFCs with Briggs. They had deployed together, drank together, and lived together for the two years they had spent at Lejeune. They hadn't been promoted with Briggs because both had incurred disciplinary infractions. Golubski and Weinman were the low men on the totem pole having just graduated from boot camp and basic infantry training. They split up the work. Two men to a jeep with Briggs floating back and forth.

"I've always wondered why we have to do this shit rather than the motor pool flunkies," Newcombe asked. He wasn't in the best of moods. He usually drank too much on weekends, so Monday was not his best day.

"They are our jeeps Newk. The mechanics don't know shit about the radios," Briggs responded.

"Well I don't know shit about engines but here I am checking the oil and cleaning off the carburetor or whatever this thing is. I didn't join the Marine Corps to be a fucking gear head. They should be doing this crap." He had his head under the open hood.

Grumbling was to be expected. It was part of being a Marine. Everyone did it. No one listened. The work got done.

"Did you go to D.C. this weekend?" Newcombe asked.

"Yeah. I saw Quinlan and Boyce. They're at Quantico now. I connected with them and we hit the bars in Georgetown Saturday. The place was crawling with hotties."

Quinlan and Boyce had served their two years in an infantry battalion and got transferred to Quantico, the sprawling Marine base south of Washington, to serve the last year of their enlistment.

"I stayed overnight in their barracks. They are with some cushy training battalion. Not exactly sure what they do every day, but they can hardly wait to kiss the crotch goodbye."

"So, is that it? That's all you got to tell us. C'mon man. We sat around the barracks all weekend shining shoes and cleaning guns."

"Rifles." Briggs corrected Newcombe on his terminology. There was an old boot camp riddle that reinforced it.

"This is your rifle." You held up your weapon.

"This is my gun." You grabbed your man parts.

"This is for shooting." Holding up your weapon.

"This is for fun." Grabbing your man parts.

"Yeah. Whatever. I call them guns just to piss off the lifers. Besides, how do you know I wasn't talking about cleaning my gun?" Newcombe grabbed his crotch. "I did succeed in getting shit faced at Jazzland. That was the highlight of my weekend."

"Did you ride the comet back," Briggs asked.

"Yeah. It wasn't too bad. There were a couple of young PFC's who were totally wasted in the back, but they were sleeping so the gate guards didn't fuck with 'em too much."

"I met this girl over the weekend that I liked. Actually, I met her last month on a bus when Mitchell and I were coming back from Myrtle Beach. College girl."

Newcombe didn't respond while he was reading the oil level on the jeep dipstick.

"Hmmm. College girl. Moving on up these days Briggsy?"

"Yeah man. Talking to a girl that knows how to read is a significant improvement over trying to talk with a bunch of Marines with the combined I Q of a turtle."

"Are you going to see her again?"

"Yeah. I'm thinking of making a trip up there next weekend." Briggs realized that he had not made a date with Brenda and he would need to do that before committing to the drive to Fredericksburg. Plus, Quantico wasn't exactly a hotel for Marines looking for a weekend bunk although he figured he would probably be able to work something out there.

Other than the usual Wednesday morning hike of about ten miles it was a light training week. The focus of each workday was spent on equipment maintenance and inventory. Inspections were becoming more frequent.

With personnel rotation dates having occurred in the summer, almost half of the battalion was new, officers and enlisted. The junior NCO's like Briggs were being counted on to step up and help train the new troops.

The comm platoon had to also break in a new commanding officer, First Lieutenant David Hotchkiss. He had gotten his commission through the Naval ROTC at Georgia Tech where he had played football. He came off as a gung-ho Marine.

Hotchkiss had spent the previous year as a platoon commander in one of the infantry line companies. The move to the Comm Platoon was a step up once he was promoted from 2nd Lieutenant to the silver bar of a First Lieutenant.

Thursday night after work Briggs got in line to use one of the two pay phones outside the mess hall. The lines got longer as the weekend approached. Sunday night was the worst because all the homesick Marines called their mommas that night.

Most of the men in front of him were quick with their calls conscious of the fact that the line was growing longer. He waited about 10 minutes. Instead of the usual collect call he made home to his parents, he had to have enough coins to call Fredericksburg and hope that he wouldn't be kept waiting too long for Brenda to pick up the phone. He had a couple dollars of coins in his pocket ready to go.

"Mary Leonard McCormick Residence Hall. May I help you?"

"Brenda Kiley please. She's in room 243." At least he had gotten that piece of information from her.

There were a few clicks and then silence. For a moment he thought he had been disconnected.

"Hello." It was Brenda.

"Hey. Brenda. It's me John."

Silence. "John?"

"Yeah. John Briggs. Marine Corps. John Briggs." Why did I say a stupid thing like that, he thought? "How ya doing?"

"Oh John. Hi. Fine." She seemed surprised.

"I was thinking of heading up your way again this weekend and wondered if we could get together?" This was the moment of truth. The question that all men hated to ask hoping not to be turned down. If she said "no" he wasn't quite sure what his next move should be.

"Sure. That would be fine. I'm staying on campus this weekend. What did you have in mind? I do have some tests I'm studying for, so I need to spend some time at that. But, yeah. I would like to see you again."

For that answer Briggs would have driven to Los Angeles and back. A trip to Fredericksburg was only five hours.

They agreed to meet Saturday afternoon. She mentioned showing him some of the Civil War battlefields in the area and then dinner. They tried to talk some more about their plans but were interrupted at the end of his original three minutes of telephone time by the mechanical voice of the AT&T operator: "please deposit 75 cents for the next 3 minutes." He had to fumble around inserting quarters while Brenda waited patiently on the other end.

"Klung. Klung. Klung." The quarters dropped. He heard her amused laugh on the other end.

"Sorry about that. All we have here are pay phones. I've got about a thousand guys lined up behind me all getting pissed off that I'm taking up so much time. I've run out of coins now, so this will be it. We have two minutes."

They wrapped up things with 12 seconds to go if his watch was correct. "See you Saturday."

CHAPTER 5

September 1965
Camp Lejeune, North Carolina

It was Friday night. Staff Sergeant Ernie Lincoln and Gunnery Sergeant Abraham Ford were busy getting shitfaced at the NCO club.

The war in South Vietnam was beginning to heat up and lifers like Lincoln and Ford knew they would eventually be headed in that direction. At least they hoped they would. This is what they trained for. This was where they earned their pay.

The first ground troops committed to the war, from the 9th Marine Expeditionary Force, landed in country March 8. By all accounts, they were kicking ass and taking names. At least that's what the generals were telling the press.

Stateside Marines were of two minds: get the hell out of the crotch before getting sent across the big pond, or just the opposite for the career Marines who saw honor, prestige, and promotion in the war. No one ever saw themselves as getting killed or being the victim of disfiguring war wounds. It had been twelve years since the war in Korea ended and the opportunities to add combat ribbons had since been few and far between.

Additional Army and Marine units had recently joined the fight. The buildup was going full blast. The Army was given responsibility for the south and central sectors of the country while the Marines were responsible for I-Corps, which was the north end of the country up to the DMZ and the border with North Vietnam.

U.S. casualty counts were beginning to rise but were always reported as being significantly less than that of the VC. Media reports quoting field commanders made it sound like a lopsided win for our side.

In August, the Marine Corps had extended all enlistment discharge dates by four months, so they could build up the number of troops needed to meet the demands of Vietnam while maintaining their other missions around the world.

The troops who most coveted the title of ex-Marine were anxious to get out and restart their civilian lives. Many were bitter about having to serve four additional months.

"Have you talked to Sierra recently," Ford asked.

"Nah. She's back home in Chicago with her mom. She can stay there for all I give a shit. When she was here, she was just giving me shit all the time. Who needs it?"

"Life in the crotch is tough on wives, and kids." Ford was trying to be sympathetic to his buddy whose marriage had been on the rocks for some time.

"The only kids I got aren't with Sierra so she ain't got nothing to be bitchin' about there. She keeps getting her allotment. Nothin' I can do about that unless we get divorced."

"You figure she's fucking around on you?"

"I don't know. She gets back to the old neighborhood and anything could start cooking. I was never quite sure what the hell she was doing when she was down here with me."

Ernie and Sierra Lincoln had known each other as teenagers growing up in Chicago. Their marriage occurred after they had both been through other relationships and had children with other partners. She moved down to Lejeune to be with Ernie after they got married in 1963. She worked at a few jobs in Jacksonville and on the base but hadn't stayed long at anything. Money was tight and became a constant source of tension between them. His twice a year deployments didn't help the relationship.

"If the crotch wanted you to have a wife, they would have issued you one," Lincoln mumbled between sips of beer. "I should have known better. I've seen enough fucked up marriages to know that it's a tough road to travel.

"I'm thinking of putting in my papers to get over to 'Nam, get out of here and just tell Sierra she can go fuck herself."

"Yeah man. I got you. Figure we'll all be going soon enough," Ford responded. "We got to get these troopers trained. There aren't that many old timers around like you and me who have seen the dark end of a tracer heading in your direction.

"Look at some of these officers we're getting now. They look like they're twelve years old. And they act like it. Not sure I want to go scuffling around the bush with some of these kids leading the action."

"I know what you mean," Lincoln responded. "Some of them are real virgins that need to get their cherries busted."

They were both silent for a few minutes, nursing their beers, looking around the club to see who they knew and giving thought to their lot in life.

"They ain't all fucked up though," Lincoln said. "We got this new C O in the comm platoon. Hotchkiss. Ex-football player. Georgia Tech. He seems like a good guy. Has his head screwed on right and not trying to act like he knows everything. Said he was relying on me to keep running the platoon."

"Yeah. Right. I've heard that before," Ford said. "Southern white boy? Be careful there, Linc. You know how that can end up. Once he gets his feet wet, he'll think you don't know shit."

"Yeah. I know what you mean. We'll see what happens."

They fell into a silence that lasted for a couple minutes. Ford had a habit of picking off the label of his beer while he drank. The label was usually gone at about the same time as the beer.

"How about we get a couple more," Ford said. "My turn."

"Yeah man. Why not. I'm drinking Bud tonight."

They accomplished their goal of being shitfaced by about 9:30 p.m. – that would be 2130 military time. Ford was the Alpha Company gunnery sergeant in 1/8. They lived in the barracks across a road and a small parade ground from 3/8. They could walk most of the distance together before heading off to their own units.

As staff NCO's they had their own rooms. Officially they weren't supposed to drink alcohol in the barracks, but no one enforced that rule. Many staff NCOs kept a fifth of their favorite liquor, Jim Beam, Johnnie Walker, Early Times, or whatever was on sale at the PX, for nighttime sipping.

It wasn't an easy life for staff NCOs who were like dormitory proctors in college, being responsible for a bunch of 19-year-old Marines who had problems with drinking, were homesick for their girlfriends and family, and lacked basic judgement in how to conduct their lives.

CHAPTER 6

October 1965
0430 Hours
Camp Lejeune, North Carolina

"Okay Marines – Drop your cocks and grab your socks! Let's move it. You got one hour to grab some chow, take a shit and whatever else you got to do. We kick off at 0600 hours.

"Ten miles today – full packs, rifles, helmets – the whole shebang. No laggards. Everyone on the company street ten minutes before we step off."

Staff Sergeant Ernie Lincoln had been awake since 0300. It was part of his DNA. He knew he needed to kick some butt to get his troops out of the sack, fed, clean the squad bay, conduct an equipment check and get the Marines ready to march. This was the beginning of the fall training period which included the weekly forced march.

His voice had a drill field quality which served him well in getting attention.

He flipped the lights on full blast and walked up and down the center aisle of the squad bay. It was time for the 36 Marines of the Communications Platoon, H&S Company, 3rd Battalion, 8th Marine Regiment to get to work.

"The mess hall is open. If you're eating breakfast, do it now. I want everyone on the grinder by zero five fifty.

"Corporal Briggs. Your team is responsible for final squad bay cleanup. I want it spic and span before you head out. Make it happen."

Lincoln had met the night before with the junior NCOs, so everyone knew their job in advance. But it was the responsibility of the platoon sergeant to remind them and ride herd to make sure it got done.

The platoon was divided into three sections – the radio team, the wiremen, and the message center operators.

The Marines who slept in the top bunks kept their cigarettes on top of their wall lockers and started reaching for them before they even had their eyes open. The Marines in the lower bunks needed to roll out of the sack before reaching for their tobacco fix.

Everyone had their field gear ready to go the night before. There was no time in the morning for anything other than a last-minute adjustment. The mess hall was serving the traditional chipped beef and cream known as "shit on a shingle." The troops needed to get over there quickly if they were going to put anything in their stomachs before their morning hike.

Briggs had preassigned each man in his six-man radio team a job for the morning cleanup. Everyone was expected to do their jobs as directed but it was still the NCOs job to make sure it happened. There were the ones like Hal Parker who didn't need any pushing. He was a low maintenance lance corporal who acted like a gunnery sergeant.

Then there were the 10 percenters, like PFC Danny Jetland, a wise ass from Detroit. Jetland moved just fast enough to stay out of trouble but never exerted more effort than the required minimum.

In the philosophy of the Marine Corps, there were always 10 percent of the troops who didn't get it, or just didn't want to get it. They were the ones that had to be pushed and threatened. Ironically, the 10 percenters often were skilled at their own MOS (Military Occupational Specialty), but just didn't like dealing with the Mickey Mouse of the Marine Corps and resisted it as much as possible.

In Jetland's case, he was one of the best CW (Morse Code) operators in the platoon. When there was a radio net that needed the best and fastest operator it was Jetland that the NCOs relied upon. They overlooked his otherwise shitty attitude about all other things military to take advantage of his skill set as a communicator.

At 0550 hours the sun was just beginning to make its appearance. The sky was pink in the east and still dark in the west. The North Carolina Piedmont was going to experience a clear but hot and humid day. Hikes were scheduled in the morning while it was still relatively cool.

Miraculously, everyone was in place on time and standing tall on the grinder in front of the company barracks when Staff Sergeant Lincoln called them to attention. They were in three rows of twelve men each. There was some early morning grumbling but that ceased quickly.

"Atten-hut! Dress Right, Dress!" The Marines shuffled into position straightening up the ranks.

"Ready, Front."

Commands as old as time and understood by all soldiers in all armies. It was the military equivalent of "On your mark. Get Set. Go."

Lieutenant Hotchkiss had been standing off to the side waiting for Lincoln to call the troops to attention and turn them over to him.

"Sir. Comm platoon ready." Lincoln pulled off a smart salute.

Hotchkiss stepped in front of Lincoln and returned the salute. Hotchkiss took a deep breath and in a command voice ordered "Right Face!"

He walked to the front of the ranks which were now facing the direction they were headed and ordered "March."

As Hotchkiss moved out Lincoln moved up with him and shouted, "two columns!" The Marines merged three ranks into two with a bit of shuffling like cars merging to get around a construction zone. It was accompanied by the sounds of clanking helmets, shifting packs and weapons being readjusted before the pace picked up and everyone found their space. Each column took one side of the road.

Hotchkiss was just under 6 feet tall, so the pace he set was manageable for everyone. Marines dreaded following a leader who was 6 feet 6 inches tall with a stride to match. That was murder on the troops in the rear.

At first there was a little chatter between them but that ceased quickly as they began to experience the exertion of the hike. No one walked into battle anymore. This wasn't the Civil War when entire armies walked from Michigan to Virginia, fought the enemy and moved on to another battle.

Since World War I armies rode in trucks to the battlefield. But military tradition demanded that soldiers were fit and capable of a brisk walk before the battle began.

Hotchkiss and Lincoln had planned to complete the ten miles in under three hours. That was a comfortable but steady pace on the side of paved roads leading out of Main Side Lejeune into the boonies and the training areas.

Briggs and Mitchell had been assigned the job of rear road guards wearing bright colored vests, so drivers would slow down and pass carefully. They liked this assignment as they could adjust their own pace to the Marines who continually fell back and then had to hurry to catch up with the main body. It was almost a leisurely walk for them compared to the rest of the troops.

"What's going on with the chick in D.C." Mitchell asked.

"It's going good man. I've been up there a couple times now to see her. First time I stayed at Quantico with Boyce and Quinlan. Last time I stayed in a motel down the road from her college. That gets a bit pricey for a corporal, so I need to find some alternative housing if I continue to make that trip.

"She's invited me to some sorority shindig next month. I think she wants me to wear my uniform. She's got it in her mind that I'm going to show up in dress blues. Hell, I don't own any dress blues. Do you?"

"Nah. Haven't had any on since my boot camp photo. And if you recall they only gave you the jacket and the barracks cover to make you look like a Marine for the photo op."

They heard a truck coming from behind. They turned and waved to make sure the driver saw them. After the truck slowly passed between the columns, they continued their conversation.

"That should be an experience," Mitchell said. "Sounds like the high school prom. Maybe you'll get into it with some of those college frat boys. Are you banging her yet?"

Briggs didn't like the sound of that. It was offensive but he decided to ignore the comment. It's the way young men talked to each other. He knew Mitchell didn't mean any disrespect.

"Nah. We haven't gotten to that point. We're still trying to figure each other out."

They were about 45 minutes into the hike when Hotchkiss and Lincoln led the column onto a dirt road heading through the piney woods. They would not encounter any auto traffic here, but Briggs and Mitchell still needed to stay alert. The day had begun to heat up and the sweat dripped from under their helmets.

When the columns were clear of the paved road Staff Sergeant Lincoln announced a ten-minute break. Everyone was limited to two full canteens. They were warned to practice water discipline and were expected to finish the hike with one full canteen left.

For most of the experienced troops this was not a problem. They monitored the first-year Marines who wanted to gulp as much as they could at each rest stop.

This was an easy hike, but there was always a guessing game as to who might drop out blaming blisters or the heat. The last hike they were joined by the battalion Sergeant Major who was 20 years older than the average trooper and at least 50 pounds overweight. His career had consisted primarily of administrative positions and his commanding officers had been lax on making him be in shape. It was rumored that the battalion CO had made him make the hike despite the Sergeant Major's protests and claims that he had too much paperwork to finish.

He lasted a bit over one hour. When he had fallen back with the rear road guards and showed little ability to keep up, he was allowed to ride in the medical jeep. If the battalion ever had to go to war it would be without Sergeant Major Grimes.

After the break Hotchkiss and Lincoln picked up the pace. They finished the next two miles in less than a half hour then turned the columns towards Main Side. With three miles to go they took one more five-minute break. Then they kicked into gear, finishing the ten miles in less than two and half hours.

Lincoln got the platoon into formation while Hotchkiss disappeared to wherever it was that officers go when NCOs take command.

"Atten-hut. Right Face – Right. Ready - Front. At ease!"

"Good job. We did it in two hours and 22 minutes. Clean your rifles and field gear. Go to chow. Get haircuts, go to the laundry or whatever else you need to do. We'll expect to see you at the comm shack by 1400 hours."

"Atten-hut. Dismissed."

CHAPTER 7

October 1965
Camp Lejeune, North Carolina

The intensive fall training period culminated in inspections and skills competitions between all the units in the Second Marine Division. Fitness reports for officers were based on their outfit's performance and readiness.

The officers pushed the NCOs who in turn pushed the troops. People and equipment had to be in tip top shape. Each day a training schedule was posted which began with group calisthenics. The younger Marines were already in good shape. They laughed at the older sergeants who had spent more time in the NCO club than they had exercising, and now were tasked with leading the group physical training.

Certain days were committed to cleaning personal weapons and 782 (field) gear. Anything that was worn out and needed replacement was reported to supply.

"Corporal Briggs! Where's Corporal Briggs?" PFC Truman Lipsky barged into the squad bay where everyone was hard at work inventorying their equipment.

Lipsky was the runner for the Comm Platoon commander. Back in boot camp the job description was a "house mouse." Because of his officious manner and his first name, Lipsky had earned the nickname President Truman.

"Yo! Right here."

"Lieutenant Hotchkiss wants to see you. Comm shack. Move your ass."

"Did you just tell me to move my ass? C'mon President Truman. Show a little more respect for an NCO."

"This is directly from the lieutenant. He wants you now." Big emphasis on the words "lieutenant" and "now". President Truman felt that the lieutenant's authority extended to him.

"Okay. You've delivered your message. Calm down and go change your Kotex. I'll be over in a few minutes. I don't think the LT will be going to war without me."

The comm shack was a Quonset hut located across the road from the barracks. Fifteen minutes after he had been summoned Briggs reported as ordered. He knocked on the wood door frame to the tiny office occupied by Lieutenant Hotchkiss.

"You wanted to see me Sir?"

Marine Corps etiquette as taught in boot camp would have required Briggs to stand at attention and state loudly: "Sir, Corporal Briggs reporting as ordered, Sir."

That was considered boot camp crap and if he was respectful in his tone most officers did not require it.

Hotchkiss weighed in at about 220 pounds. He was still at his playing weight from when he was a linebacker for the Rambling Wreck of Georgia Tech.

Sitting in the one available guest chair hunched over papers on that side of the desk was platoon Staff Sergeant Ernie Lincoln. No small man himself, he could have been a lineman. Compared to these two the office furniture looked like it was meant for children's day care.

There were no extra seats, and the office was so small there was little space for Briggs to stand. Hotchkiss looked up from the papers he was reading, then looked over at Lincoln who had also been absorbed in whatever he was reading. Hotchkiss nodded to Lincoln.

"Briggs. We've got three new troopers coming in today," Lincoln said. "All three are just back from Nam. They're down at battalion headquarters waiting to get picked up. Run down there and collect them. They've got their sea bags with them, so take one of the mites."

A Mighty Mite was a small jeep that was not as big or as good as the traditional military Jeep. They were manufactured exclusively for the Marine Corps with the idea that because of their smaller size they would fit more easily inside a helicopter. But it wasn't long before helicopters became so powerful that the smaller vehicle was unnecessary. The comm platoon had four Mighty Mites assigned to it.

"Find them racks, sheets, blankets and then over to supply for their field gear and to the armory. They all rate M-14s. One of these guys is a corporal. Do we have any extra racks in the NCO quarters?"

"Yes Sir. We have one extra bunk. Corporal Driver rotated out a couple weeks ago. No problem."

"Okay. Get on it. Make them feel loved and all that touchy feely shit that we're supposed to do these days. Fill them in on the schedule. Then get them fed and over here after noon chow. Here's the paperwork."

Briggs was dismissed with a nod. "Aye, aye, Sir." Since no one says "sir" to an NCO, Lincoln wasn't sure if Briggs was being a wise-ass or not. He let it slide.

Hotchkiss never had to utter a word. It was Lincoln's job to make sure things got done. Lieutenants tell sergeants what to do. Sergeants tell corporals what to do.

Picking up the new transfers and getting them settled was job appropriate for a newly minted corporal.

Battalion headquarters was a half mile away. When Briggs left the sun was shining. By the time he got there it had started to rain. There not being any roof on the Mighty Mite this was going to be a wet ride.

Marines reporting into a new duty station were required to wear their dress uniforms. Typically, the Marine Corps switched from summer tropical worsted to dress wool greens on October 15. It was easy for Briggs to spot the new guys. They were sitting uncomfortably with their sea bags in the headquarters lobby, waiting for their ride.

Two of them, a lance corporal, and a PFC, were in their summer uniforms. The corporal was wearing the heavier winter greens.

Briggs figured somebody was probably chewed out for wearing the wrong uniform, even though the changeover was just one day old. There was always some field grade officer or staff NCO looking to bust balls particularly with transfers. It was like an unwritten rule. Give the new guys shit.

Briggs and the corporal sat in the front seats. The lower rank guys sat on the two-fold-up seats in the back holding onto their sea bags to keep them from tumbling into the street.

Corporal Richard "Dick" Gamboney had just reenlisted for four years. He had been with 3/9 in Okinawa when they got sent to Vietnam as the first Marine combat troops in country. They landed March 8, 1965, on a beach in South Vietnam. It was an unopposed landing if one did not count the numerous local vendors selling soda pop, beach chairs and condoms. Anytime the Marines landed the public had visions of the invasion of Iwo Jima.

Lance Corporal Greg Tyson was a field radio operator. He had served with Gamboney. He still had 16 months to go on his enlistment.

PFC Frank Cash had an attitude. When Briggs tried to talk with him Cash responded with grunts and mumbles. He was not a happy camper. He had just arrived and already seemed pissed off. Cash admitted to having spent three months in Vietnam but offered nothing more.

Briggs decided to ignore Tyson and Cash while talking with Gamboney. Both being corporals, they were able to connect.

"I hear you're back from 'Nam. How was it over there?"
"The shits. Hot. Wet. Cold. Pick your poison. When the monsoons came, we were walking through three feet of mud. Temps dropped to the 40's. I know that doesn't sound cold, but everything is relative. It's cold after you get used to it being 100 degrees with 90 percent humidity."

"Any action?"

"Some incoming mortar a few times. They hit a couple planes. Mostly they just left holes in the ground. The grunts would chase 'em but Charlie was gone before you knew it. Hit & run. I was on a few patrols but nothing that got the blood pumping."

"Did you get any leave before heading here?"

"Fifteen days at home. Upstate New York. Syracuse. Give me the lowdown on what we've got here. What's the comm officer like?"

"Hotchkiss. Ex-college football player so he expects everyone to be in great shape. Nothing wrong with that. Staff Sergeant Lincoln runs things. Black guy. Korea vet. He doesn't smile much, nobody's buddy, but he's fair with everyone. Knows his shit in the field.

"I'll get you guys settled. You can get out of those wet uniforms and change into utilities. We'll hit supply and the armory then make it to noon chow. Lieutenant Hotchkiss wants to see you at 1400. Let's meet in the barracks at 1345 and I'll walk you over."

Hotchkiss did the basic howdy-do: "Welcome. Glad you are here. Staff Sergeant Lincoln will fill you in on the details." He nodded in Lincoln's direction.

"First things first. I know you guys just got back from Nam and you might be feeling like salty war veterans. I don't want to see any of that big timer attitude bullshit. Any experience you picked up over there that you can share with the other troops, good. Glad to have it. But, don't act like you just won a war because so far, we haven't done jack shit. This war is just starting. You stay in the crotch long enough you'll be going back."

Lincoln outlined the daily work schedules and expectations. Gamboney took notes like an NCO is taught to do on a small notebook that fit into the top pocket of his utility jacket. Tyson and Cash just nodded. Briggs watched their body language trying to determine what was sticking and what wasn't.

Gamboney had more seniority than Briggs so he was assigned to be the platoon radio chief. Briggs would be his assistant.

Tyson was assigned to the message center. Cash was a wireman. They went their separate ways.

After work and evening chow, Briggs took Gamboney to the NCO club. Mitchell, who had also made corporal the last promotion period, went with them. U.S. combat troops had been in Vietnam for less than a year, so every returning Marine was like a rock star to those who hadn't gone yet. There was a sense of awe about these guys even though they were just Marines. No heroes among them.

It was still early when they got to the club. Budweiser was the beer of choice that night. Briggs and Mitchell interrogated Gamboney on all the elements of Vietnam. He had spent his entire time in or around the Danang Air Base.

"Shoot anyone?"

"Fuck no. Never saw anybody to shoot. My rifle was as clean when I left as it was when I got there."

"What was the weather like?"

"Wet. Sunny. Hot. Cold. Basically, the place is the shits."

"Where did you live?"

"Tents. Big tents with wooden floors. Just like we had at Camp Matthews."

Camp Matthews was the rifle range serving Marine Corps Recruit Depot San Diego until it was turned into a state university in the mid-60s.

"On hot days, the sun would beat on them and by mid-morning it was like being in a sauna. You couldn't stay there. You needed to go to one of the communication bunkers, or a hangar or one of the other open shelters to cool off.

"Lots of critters and rodents. We stood guard twenty-four, seven around the perimeter. We did some patrolling outside the base to the south and to the west. There was some open territory in those directions. Otherwise, Danang city was right outside the fence line.

"The officers seemed to be going bug fuck nuts wanting to find some action for us. Most of the time we were just standing watches around the base perimeter."

"It all sounds pretty tame," Briggs commented. "Waiting for the war to start. Right?"

"Yeah. We didn't do shit. The Army seemed to be fighting more of a war down south toward Saigon. On our patrols, we did encounter a few ARVN units around Danang. They always had U.S. advisors. Almost always Army. I think I saw one Marine advisor.

"Honestly? The place is a shit hole. Not sure why the hell we are there."

CHAPTER 8

October 1965
Fredericksburg, Virginia

Vietnam War Timeline: Between October 21, 1957, and June 6, 1965, 667 Americans would be immortalized on Panel 1-E of The Vietnam Veterans Memorial Wall. It took only four more months until the end of October 1965 for Panel 2-E to reach capacity with 704 additional names.

The Tarheel Truck Oasis in Wilson, North Carolina, was the first pit stop after leaving Camp Lejeune. It took two hours to travel 83 miles. It was the most direct route to hook up with I-95. From there to Washington it was all Interstate.

Briggs picked up two other riders at the Lejeune Circle to share the expense. They were going all the way to D.C. which meant he agreed to drive an additional 100 miles to D.C. and back to Fredericksburg. But the $50 was worth it to him.

They would have to catch a ride back on their own Sunday night with a different Lejeune bound driver. There was an unofficial pickup spot in Washington at 14ᵗʰ Street and Pennsylvania Avenue where Marines with cars could find riders to share the costs. If one did not know better that corner on Sunday night looked like a hookers' stroll except it was all Marines. It was a transportation system that had evolved over the years. No one ever seemed too concerned about not being able to find a ride back in time. If anything, there was a shortage of riders, not drivers.

Once they left Lejeune there was a minimum of talk between the passengers. The radio replaced conversation. Music of the 50s and 60s was what they liked - Motown – Marvin Gaye, the Supremes, the Temptations. WABC out of New York with Cousin Brucie spinning the disks was the station of choice.

Briggs' two passengers were lance corporal grunts from 6th Marines. One of them lived in the D.C. area and was taking his buddy home for the weekend. The 6th Marines were authorized to wear the French Fourragere on their uniforms. It is a braided rope worn around the left shoulder that was presented to the 5th and 6th Marines during World War I for their actions in the famous battle of Belleau Wood.

Although those who wear the award are proud of their regiment's history, other Marines refer to it derisively as a pogey bait rope. Pogey bait being the term commonly used in the military to describe candy. Others suggested that it was worn to indicate a Marine infected with a venereal disease.

This was Briggs' fourth trip to Fredericksburg. He had stayed overnight the first couple weekends at Quantico. The last trip he stayed at a motel outside of town. The extra trip dollars he got from his riders paid for the room. Brenda stayed with him one night. They cuddled and kissed but that was as far as it had gone.

There had been weekly phone calls and a couple letters exchanged. This weekend Brenda's sorority was having their fall shindig and Briggs was her date. This was the first time for him to attend a formal college event. They did not have these things at Kellogg Community College in Battle Creek.

She asked him to wear his dress uniform. Of course, she had in mind the classy dress blues that the Marine Corps loves to show off in every publicity photo, but that few Marines ever own or wear. No need for a grunt. Nothing ceremonial in his job description.

Briggs asked around to see if anyone in the platoon owned a set of blues he could borrow but came up empty. He decided his winter greens would have to do. He spent extra time during the week polishing and buffing and clipping Irish Pennants (dangling threads). He treated it like an inspection.

The trip from Lejeune to Washington, D.C. took 6 hours. After he backtracked to Fredericksburg he checked into his room at the Colonial Travel Lodge shortly after midnight. He hit the rack and fell to sleep immediately.

Briggs woke up at 5:37 a.m. reveille at Lejeune was 0530 so this was like sleeping in. It was automatic. After more than three years of military life he was programmed to wake up at the same time each day regardless of how much sleep he had.

Briggs and Brenda had pre-arranged to meet for breakfast but that was not until 9 a.m. so he had lots of time to kill. He decided to go for a run on the empty streets of Fredericksburg. He hoped he would not be hassled by the local police who may think he was a criminal rather than a Marine on his early morning jog.

George's Grill was a diner located just off campus within walking distance of Brenda's dorm. Briggs' figured it was named after George Washington. Everything around there seemed to be named after George or someone in his family.

Brenda was waiting for him in a window booth when he arrived. She already had a cup of coffee in front of her.

"Where you been sleepy head? I thought Marines were always the first up. I was beginning to think that I got stood up for a breakfast date."

Briggs looked at his watch. It was 9:02. He was two minutes late.

"Hey, it's my day off. I decided to sleep in. You would make a great drill sergeant." They had reached the point in their relationship that the exchange of kisses felt right.

"Are you ready for tonight? This is going to be a first, you know. The word is out that I'm bringing a Marine to 'Belles and Beaus'."

"Belles and what?"

"Beaus. You are my beau. That is southern talk for boyfriend. Belles and Beaus is the theme of our fall sorority formal."

"Okay, if you say so. Sounds pretty corny to me."

"I agree. It is kind of stupid but there's got to be a theme. I think a sorority at every college in the country uses the same ones."

Briggs had been uncomfortable about this since she had invited him. He knew he would stick out among all the fraternity twats. But he did not want to tell Brenda no.

"You're sure about this right? You want me showing up in uniform. I could go out this afternoon and buy a suit. I probably wouldn't have enough money left for gas back to Lejeune, but I'll figure something out."

"No. I like you as a Marine. You are my Marine. If somebody doesn't like it, that's their tough shit."

"Whooee! Talking tough girl. Do they allow that language at Mary Washington College?"

The war in Vietnam had been heating up for more than a year. The American public was becoming increasingly aware of the consequences with lines being drawn and opinions hardening on both sides of the argument.

Once boots were on the ground the previous March, the profile of the Marine Corps had become identified with the war. Marines had become targets of protesters. Things had gotten ugly.

College campuses had become more radical and students were actively protesting the war. Places like the University of Wisconsin, Columbia University and the University of California were hotbeds. ROTC units found themselves in the crosshairs of protest groups and were needing to walk a fine line trying to lower their profiles on campus.

As they ate breakfast Brenda tried to assure Briggs that he was going to have a good time. There was nothing to worry about. An all-women's college in Fredericksburg, Virginia, was not exactly the forefront of radicalism.

"Our student manual still requires us to wear skirts, hose and collared blouses at all times while on campus. No smoking. No drinking. And heaven forbid, no premarital sex.

"One girl last year was suspended when she showed up braless at the student union. That sent the deans up the wall."

"Won't there be some anti-military people there?"

"Most of them won't even know that you are in the military. They'll probably think you're a bus driver."

"Oh, thanks. That's great. Just the impression I'm trying to make."

He told her that he was not wearing dress blues. She frowned and pretended to be disappointed. He assured her how military he would look in his greens.

"Do you have all those little ribbon things on your chest that you get for being brave?" He knew she was mocking him.

"I've never been in any battles, so other than a good conduct medal and my rifle and pistol badges the answer is no. You'll have to take me as I am."

"Can't you run up to Quantico and just buy some real quick for the night? I've been telling everyone what a war hero you are." She was continuing to pull his chain just to get a reaction. He still felt it required a response.

"No. That I cannot do. Wearing unauthorized medals and ribbons is frowned upon, and in fact, it is a violation of the military code of conduct. You will just have to take me for what I am. Accept the fact that I'm showing up at all. This isn't exactly my crowd."

Since Briggs had been in 3/8, the battalion had come close to action three times in the past two years. But no medals or ribbons were authorized.

The battalion was deployed during the Cuban Missile Crisis, but that was settled before they ever got off their ships. Then 3/8 was undergoing jungle training in the Panama Canal Zone in January 1964 when anti-American riots broke out.

They were kept on standby at Coco Solo Naval Base for six weeks. The only hostile action they saw was with other Marines during training exercises in learning how to quell a mob.

In April 1965, the U.S. sent 40,000 troops, Marines, and army, to the Dominican Republic to stop a government coup. Thirty-one U.S. servicemen were killed in action so this was no minor dustup. However, 3/8 having just returned from deployment was spared the trip.

"Oh, you're being so serious. Lighten up. You'll have a good time. You can show everyone your tattoo. I'm sure you'll be the only one there with an eagle, globe and anchor."

"Alright. Enough. You got me." He knew she was just poking fun at him. He was trying to be a good sport, but it didn't do much to relieve his anxiety about the differences in their social status, a topic which they had so far ignored during their young relationship.

It was a sunny and brisk fall day. If the campus had been the University of Virginia, or back home in Ann Arbor, everyone would have been getting ready for a football game. There was nothing of that sort at Mary Washington College.

After breakfast they took a walk on the campus. Brenda nuzzled up to Briggs, shivering in the brisk fall air. She pointed out the various buildings, dormitories, sorority houses, classrooms, gymnasium. Some buildings had historical plaques explaining the history of the campus, the Fredericksburg area and its place in both the civil and revolutionary wars.

They shared stories about their families and lives back home and what the future might look like for each of them. They wandered into downtown, found a local bookstore and spent an hour browsing.

She bought a book on the history of quilt making. He bought Battle Cry by Leon Uris. She led them into a small gallery where she gave him an introduction to Art 101, a class she had finished in her freshman year. He had never spent any time in an art gallery and did not know the first thing about it. In his home, art was something his mother could pick up at the home decorating department of Sears for less than $20.

It was obvious that Brenda had a great appreciation of the paintings and the individual artists. She took the time to patiently explain to Briggs some of the techniques the artists used. He found himself enjoying this and being more interested than he thought he would. It made her happy to see him show an interest and be impressed with her knowledge.

The countryside was splashed with fall colors, so they decided to take a drive following the Rappahannock River and touring a few of the Civil War battlefields like the Spotsylvania National Military Park.

They were a young couple enjoying getting to know each other. They shared laughs, subtle touches and quick glances at each other. Anticipation was building for both about the evening's activities.

Briggs continued to be concerned about how he would fit into the college scene. The campus clashes had become more frequent around the nation. He figured that in his uniform he would be making a statement that would not be appreciated by everyone.

Brenda did not know much about the differences between the military ranks, but she was aware that corporals don't usually date sorority girls. Most of her friends' boyfriends who were in the military were officers. She did not want to admit it to herself, but she was worried about how her friends would accept and treat Briggs. Then she would put it out of her mind by telling herself that she didn't give a shit. She liked him and that was all that mattered.

CHAPTER 9

October 1965 – Saturday Night
Fredericksburg, Virginia

Belles & Beaus was held at the Heritage Oaks Golf Club about 5 miles from campus. The room decorations reminded Briggs of a wedding rather than a sorority formal, then again maybe that is how it was meant to look.

Brenda looked terrific in her formal dress. Her blond hair was swept up in a way that reminded him of Audrey Hepburn. Brenda's blue green eyes and crinkly smile mesmerized him. When she laughed it was as if the world laughed with her. She was without doubt the hottest girl he had ever dated.

Briggs was feeling on top of his game as well. His dress greens were immaculate. Expert rifle and pistol badges gleaming. Brass and dress shoes shined and ready for inspection. He looked like a recruiting poster Marine. The only ribbon he was authorized to wear was for good conduct, referred to by Marines as "three years of undetected crime." He decided that one puny ribbon not awarded for anything heroic was best left in a drawer. Otherwise, it would just draw questions that he did not want to answer.

A cocktail hour then dinner and dancing. All that was missing was a bride and groom. Pre-dinner music was provided by a trio – a piano, violin and a clarinet. There did not seem to be any restrictions on drinking.

Younger sorority sisters and their dates who were obviously under-age were being served by the black waiters and waitresses that roamed through the crowd with trays of wine and champagne.

Briggs' first reaction was that this was all too grown up, hoity toity and snooty tooty for him. He had worked for a summer as a bus boy at the Lakeview Country Club in Battle Creek. Employees were required to use a separate entrance. He figured he was now the first person from his family to have entered a country club through the front door. He felt he should be working the room as a waiter not attending as a guest.

He recalled the division he had felt between members and employees. Other than the fact that he got a paycheck and good tips, he often felt like he was working at the big house in the antebellum south. Most of the adult employees, other than supervisors, were black. Most of the members were white.

Other than private club memberships, Battle Creek is a racially diverse community with a history of supporting African Americans back to the days of the underground railroad. The famous abolitionist and women's rights activist Sojourner Truth lived and died in Battle Creek. Her gravesite is a tourist attraction.

Briggs liked Brenda a lot, and there was no way he was going to screw this up. He would be on his best behavior. She had popped the $100 for the two of them to attend. All it cost him was the hotel room and dry cleaning his dress greens which had to be done anyway before the next inspection.

As she introduced him to her friends, he thought he could feel the stares he got, particularly from the college boys. He wasn't sure if he was being admired, despised or just a curiosity. He knew he was also getting the once over from Brenda's girlfriends who were curious about her Marine. Corporals did not usually make the cut with Mary Washington College women.

This social event required a lot of small talk, which was not necessarily his strong suit. He found it easier to ask questions acting like he was interested in them. If he could keep them talking about themselves he could avoid talking about himself. Whatever they wanted to know about him, his uniform said it.

He saw two other men in uniform. One was a cadet from the Virginia Military Institute who was the date of one of the younger sorority sisters. He was a couple years younger than Briggs and other than a polite nod, they paid each other no mind. The cadet's uniform was adorned with way too many badges, patches and even a Fourragere. As a military school student, he had not done anything other than learn how to ride a horse and shine his shoes.

The other was an Army Second Lieutenant wearing his formal army officer blues. Briggs figured he had probably been commissioned after graduation from West Point or one of the other academies the previous spring. He would not be earning his first lieutenant's bars until he served 18 months of active duty.

Briggs wondered if he would be an asshole and expect him to salute. Army tradition requires indoor salutes. Marines do not. He was covered by his service traditions. Nevertheless, he had run into enough high testosterone new lieutenants who wanted to break balls and were not above creating an issue about it.

They were about the same age, but Briggs had three years of service behind him including a couple of deployments to the Caribbean and Mediterranean. He was feeling much more the saltier warrior.

When dinner was to be served the waiters moved through the room ringing chimes. The lights were blinked. Conversation around the room dropped and everyone politely moved into another room all looking for their assigned seats designated with printed tent cards.

"How's it going so far Corporal Briggs," Brenda whispered to him. She squeezed his hand and pulled herself closer to him holding onto his bicep with her other hand. He instinctively tightened the muscle making her laugh. He escorted her into the dining area.

She was keeping a close eye on this exercise in intercultural relationships. She knew it was not a comfortable setting for Briggs, but the more she was with him the more she liked him. Her friends had all been polite and several had remarked to her on how good-looking he was. She was feeling more comfortable as the evening progressed.

Luck of the draw, they ended up at the same table of eight with Lieutenant Brandon Hayes, West Point Class of 1965. They nodded to each other, made a quick introduction of themselves and their dates and began small talk.

"I guess they felt it was important to keep us grunts in the same corner, so we don't start trouble," Hayes said with a conspiratorial smile. He was obviously trying to keep things informal and establish a bond. Briggs appreciated that.

"Third Battalion, Eighth Marines. Camp Lejeune. Where are you stationed Lieutenant?"

Briggs wanted to keep the conversation at a tone where he did not have to call him "sir." It was not necessary. Hayes took care of that awkwardness for him.

"Unless you feel some military compulsion to do so, please do not call me Lieutenant, Sir, or any of that other military bullshit. Brandon is fine. I know, Brandon sounds like a fruity name. Nothing I could do about it. The tradition goes back a long time in my family. Every generation has a Brandon. I'm not only Brandon, I'm Brandon the 4th." He paused and took a sip, or maybe it was more of a gulp, of his drink.

"82nd Airborne. Fort Bragg. Same part of the country as Lejeune. Fayetteville, N C. Shithole of the Piedmont."

Briggs laughed. Maybe this guy's okay, he thought to himself.

"How come you're not wearing your jump wings?" Briggs had never known an airborne soldier not to be sporting his wings. He figured they put those on before they put on their underwear.

"The pin creates holes in the uniform. These uniforms are so fucking expensive every time you wear it you end up spending a fortune to repair it. I am just praying that I don't get soup on the fucking tunic.

"Plus, I didn't want to junk it up with a lot of pinks and greens, not that I have any. Nobody here gives a shit. Ashley insisted that I wear my uniform." He nodded at his date, a hot strawberry blond who was falling out of the top of her dress as she was leaning over to talk to one of her sorority sisters.

"I would rather be wearing a suit. I don't want to get into a hassle with some liberal long-haired fraternity boy shit head. But, then again, if this turns her on..." He flipped his head and eyebrows towards Ashley.

"Besides, I think jumping out of a perfectly good airplane before it lands is really a stupid thing to do. The West Point officer corps expects this to be one of the rights of passage. Airborne training in Year Three.

"I'm hoping to get into helicopter pilot training before too long. What about you? What's your story John?"

Briggs had never been called by his first name by an officer before. He was caught off guard.

"Three years in. Two deployments. Radio operator. I've already been extended for the Vietnam buildup so I can't get out until November '66 at the earliest. I'm not sure what I will do then. Re-enlist? Get out and go back to school? I got some time to think about it."

"Vietnam is going to be the war of our generation," Hayes said. "This shit isn't going away. I just finished up the OCS Basic School and most of the instructors had spent time over there as advisors. Their unanimous opinion is that we are in for a real shit storm."

They had kept their voices down so as not to create a flap at their table. They mutually decided they should delay any more talk of Vietnam and the military and instead start focusing on their dates. Nobody else at the table understood or cared about any of this military talk.

Appetizer, sorbet, entrée with accompaniment, another sorbet, dessert. All served by white gloved waiters and waitresses. The trio continued to play throughout. This was not a Lejeune mess hall meal.

Conversation was polite and muted. The dates of the other two sisters at the table were fraternity boys from UVA. They had driven to Fredericksburg together and even though they were drinking a lot, they indicated they were going to drive back to Charlottesville that night.

The louder of the two whose name was Jason started to rag on Briggs and Hayes about the military and how the U.S. was getting its ass kicked in Vietnam. Jason had shoulder length blonde hair and wore an earring. He had a pinched-up face with prominent teeth. Briggs thought he looked like a squirrel.

"I read about the search and destroy missions and it never sounds like they find anyone. More of our guys get killed from stepping on booby traps. Seems to me the only one getting destroyed are our own troops," he commented.

The conversation at the table became one sided as Jason got drunker and louder and continued with his lecture on military effectiveness. Both Hayes and Briggs exchanged glances a couple times but otherwise listened without comment. They both were getting pissed.

The more Jason drank the more personal and insulting he became.

"What are you guys doing here anyway wearing uniforms like some little kids playing soldier? This isn't a fucking military exercise."

His date Heather, tried to quiet him down, but he shook her off and continued to blather.

"Don't pay any attention to him. He's drunk," Brenda whispered.

"Look at that squirt over there." Jason motioned to the VMI cadet. "You think anyone would be afraid of him? Hell, they would eat him for lunch."

Then he started in on Briggs. "What are the two stripes for? What rank are you?"

"Corporal."

"Corporal? That's enlisted right? How do you get to come here and sit next to a lieutenant? Do you have to wipe his ass and shine his shoes?"

Jason laughed at his own joke. He looked around the table seeking allies. It didn't matter to him if he found any or not. He was enjoying his verbal assault on the military.

Briggs and Hayes did their best to ignore Jason who took a break and either went to the men's room or outside to puke. His date Heather and his UVA buddy Alan followed him out when he didn't return after about 10 minutes.

"Who is that guy?" Brenda asked the remaining girl of the foursome. Her name was Monica. She was looking glum.

"Blind date. Both these guys are assholes. Cost me a hundred bucks. I would rather be back in the dorm studying for my Econ 202 exam. At least my date's not drinking his brains out."

Without Jason and Alan, at the table, the conversation returned to normal. Dinner was served and eaten in leisure. Monica left the table a couple times to check on the rest of her group. She returned to report that they were all outside having a cigarette and or maybe something stronger. She wasn't sure and did not care. Her major concern was getting back to the dorm afterward because there was no way she was riding in a car with them.

Brenda assured Monica they would give her a ride.

"Whoop de do. What a great night this has turned out to be," Monica commented.

When the dancing started Jason and Heather returned for a few minutes, but it did not take long before they headed for the bar.

Music was provided by a kick ass band that could switch easily between rock and roll, country, and slow dance music. Briggs felt a bit restrained dancing in his uniform, so he took his jacket off. Hayes did the same. Technically, they were out of uniform, but it wasn't like anyone was going to report them.

The two couples switched dance partners on a few songs. Briggs appreciated the opportunity to see if Ashley's boobs would fall out of her dress when the band was playing some hard rock song by the Rolling Stones, the hot new Brit band.

Briggs limited his drinking. He had a couple glasses of wine before and during dinner. After getting sweaty from dancing he ordered a beer but promised himself this was it for the night. If he was drinking at an open bar with his Marine Corps buddies, they would all be stewed to the gills.

Jason had disappeared, although Monica's date Alan did return to their table with reports that his friend was still in the area getting more drunk, or stoned, or both. He apologized and said they were leaving for Charlottesville.

Monica and Heather could bum a ride home with other couples.

The band wrapped it up before midnight. Briggs and Brenda, along with Hayes and Ashley, headed for their cars. There was a post party-party at one of the local student's homes in town. They were headed there.

As Briggs opened the car door for Brenda, Jason suddenly appeared and grabbed the door.

"Hot shot fucking Marine. The only reason you went in the Marines is because you're too fucking dumb to get into college." Jason was slurring his words.

"You're going to go over to 'Nam and get your balls shot off. You fucking deserve it. Baby killers and all that shit."

"Calm down Jason. The night's over. Let's all go our own way," Briggs responded trying to put a cap on the confrontation.

A crowd had begun to form. Briggs saw Hayes head over from his car. Brenda had gotten into the car, but Jason would not let go of the door. Alan grabbed Jason by the arm and tried to get him to leave.

"I'm not leaving until I kick this prick's ass," Jason said. Briggs saw the punch coming too late. It caught him over his right eyebrow. He was knocked a couple steps backward which was just enough time for Jason to get off one more punch. Briggs saw this one coming and was able to block it and throw his own shot which connected with Jason's nose. Blood seemed to fly everywhere. Jason was done with one punch. He collapsed first to his knees and then rolled over on the ground.

The local police, who had been directing traffic out of the parking lot, had seen the crowd gathering and heard the shouting. Two patrolmen were at the fight scene almost immediately.

One cop pushed Briggs away and told him to put his hands on the back of his car and take a spread eagle. The other cop directed everyone to back away. Then he leaned down to check on Jason who was immobile and bleeding like a stuck pig.

Brenda had witnessed the exchange of punches from her car seat. As she tried to get out, she was told by the police to stay where she was.

Most of the crowd was silent and watching. A few witnesses tried to offer the police their version of who hit who first and why. The cops got everyone to break it up and head for their cars.

"We have it under control folks. Enjoy the rest of your night. Drive careful."

Briggs remained in position waiting to be told what to do next. Hayes stood nearby. The siren of an approaching ambulance pierced the night air.

The ambulance crew was efficient at repairing Jason's nose. They quickly got him in the ambulance along with Alan and headed for the hospital. Their dates had disappeared.

"Okay jarhead. Turn around slowly and let us see if we can figure out what happened here."

Fredericksburg Police Sergeant David Fee was a black man, standing about six feet five and weighed at least 250 pounds. Briggs figured it would be appropriate for several reasons to call him "sir."

"Well sir, this little prick decided that he didn't like me or my uniform. He had too much to drink and decided to pop me one. I was just defending myself."

"He was hassling us all night officer," Hayes offered. "Corporal Briggs just did what any of us would do under the circumstances."

"Who are you," Fee asked.

"Lieutenant Brandon Hayes. 82nd Airborne, sir."

"82nd Airborne. That don't mean shit to me," Fee said with a smile. "Like this boy here, I'm a former jarhead. But, thanks for your input Lieutenant. It's always good to have you Army boys stick up for the Marines.

"Where you stationed Marine?"

"Camp Lejeune. 8th Marines."

"Yeah. I was a cannon cocker. Did two years in artillery at Lejeune with 10th Marines.

"Okay, here's what's going to happen. I figure that little shit is going to get to the hospital, get his broken nose fixed, then he'll want to press charges or threaten to file a lawsuit or some shit like that. We have a few witnesses including our officers here on scene who saw him take the first shot. Even if they did not see it, they'll say they did. So, once he sobers up, this will all go away, as it should.

"I'm going to take your names and contact information for my report. But, Briggs my advice to you is to finish your business here in town and get back to Lejeune as soon as possible. If ass wipe gets particularly revengeful, I don't want to have to come and find you.

"Okay Corporal Briggs. Give the officer over there your contact info then beat a retreat to wherever you're headed. Semper Fi."

"Right. Thanks Sergeant. Semper Fi."

CHAPTER 10

October 1965
Fredericksburg, Virginia

After the fight Briggs took Brenda back to her dorm. It was clear that she was troubled by the whole scene and any chance of her staying with him at the hotel was somewhere between slim and none.

There was heavy tension in the car during the ride back. He tried to talk with her, to discuss the situation but her one-word answers told him all he needed to know.

He walked her to the door where she stopped and turned to him. He was not getting an invite inside. There was no kiss exchanged.

"John. I need to think about all this. I'm not used to my boyfriend getting into fistfights."

"Hey, he took the poke at me. I was just defending myself."

"I don't care. It could have been handled differently. Seeing you hit him so violently made me sick at my stomach. There was blood everywhere."

"Yeah. Well that's what happens when you fuck with the eagle." He was not sure why he said that. He had never called himself an eagle before. The metaphor just seemed to fit the moment.

"I think you and I maybe need a break for a while. Good night." She turned and went inside. Briggs stood in the night air under the building portico not sure what to do next.

He went back to his hotel, laid on the bed watching TV for about a half hour. Then he changed into civvies and walked down the street to a local bar called Goldy's.

A long bar dominated the room. A few tables were set along the wall. Two couples were at one table talking loudly and smoking cigarettes. Three men were sitting at the bar. They were each drinking alone. They looked like they had been there for a while.

Briggs sat at a stool giving himself some distance from the serious drinkers. The bartender was a stout woman who looked like she could serve as the bouncer if any trouble erupted. She stood in front of him without saying anything waiting for his order.

"Bud draft."

"I.D."

"What?"

"I.D. Gotta see it."

Briggs showed her his military I.D.

She gave it a good look. "One Bud draft coming up." She was back in less than 30 seconds with his cold beer.

"So, you're the Marine that kicked the college boy's ass tonight?"

It took Briggs a moment to process what she had just said to him.

"Uh. Yeah. I guess that was me. How do you know about that?"

"Small town. Word gets out quick. I'm Goldy Harkness. Welcome to Goldy's." She stuck out her hand. Briggs could feel a grin on his face as he took her hand, which could be described as a paw.

"The first one's on me. You might want to have a talk with the gent over there. He says he had ringside seats to the fight." She nodded to a table in the corner.

Sitting with his back to the wall was police sergeant David Fee. He was with two others who by their haircuts also looked like cops. They had changed out of uniform into civilian clothes. Briggs wondered to himself how he had missed seeing them when he first walked into the bar. It was not common in Virginia for blacks and whites to be drinking in the same bar together. Usually it was a formula for trouble, but Briggs figured no one was going to mess with Sergeant Fee.

Fee waived him over. "So, here's the new Cassius Clay," referencing the current heavyweight boxing champion. "I thought I told you to get out of town."

"It's a long ride to Lejeune. I need some sleep. You wouldn't want me to waste my room at the Colonial, would you? I'll be gone by sunrise."

Fee laughed. "You make it sound like the wild west or something. This isn't Tombstone you know. I assume you checked your gun at the door?"

"Not carrying sarge. Not driving either. I just walked down here to have a beer and give a little thought to what happened tonight."

Fee nodded at the empty seat at their table. Briggs sat down.

"I take it you're sleeping in that room by yourself."

"Yeah. I wasn't planning on that but, things didn't work out."

The cops all gave him knowing smiles.

"What's with Goldy's," Briggs asked.

"What you mean is what am I doing in here drinking with all these white boys," Fee responded.

"It's a blue bar. An off-duty cop bar. White. Brown. Black. Make no difference to Goldy. She likes all colors, especially blue.

"Now let's see if we can give you some advice on how to get your girl back." That brought laughter from the other two cops who were also ex-military. Everyone started sharing stories of their time in service as well as their failed romantic adventures.

"If you don't mind me asking, what are you doing here anyways at this lily-white rich girl school? And, your buddy is a lieutenant. The pieces of the puzzle don't seem to fit."

"Yeah, I know. I am sort of walking on the other side of the tracks here, aren't I? But I like the girl. She is a ten spot. You know what I mean?"

They nodded. "On the other side of the pond they would say: 'She numbah One G I'," one of Fee's buddies said doing a bad imitation of an Asian bar girl.

"The LT? Just met him but we connected. He had my back tonight. He's cool."

Briggs felt like he was back at the NCO club. He had two more beers before calling it a night. The cops treated.

"Not too often we buy a beer for somebody we should have arrested. We did not like that mealy-mouthed little shit that you cold cocked. So, here's to you Cassius." They all held up their glasses in salute.

"Stay out of trouble. Hope you get the girl back."

When morning came Briggs packed his suitcase, checked out and headed back to George's Grill for breakfast. Twenty-four hours had passed from when he was sitting here with Brenda. He wished she were with him again. He decided to give her a call and see if they could get together and fix things. He did not want to return to Lejeune without some closure.

There was a phone booth just outside George's. He dialed the dorm and had to go through the usual switchboard protocol asking for Brenda. He was connected to the room. When the phone rang six times, he figured no one would pick up. On ring number seven Brenda answered.

"Hey. Good morning," Briggs tried to sound cheery. "How'd you sleep?"

There was a pause before she answered. "I was wondering if you were going to call. Are you still in town?"

"Yeah. Just getting ready to leave. I am in a phone booth outside George's Grill. I missed you at breakfast." She did not respond.

"I was hoping we could get together and discuss what happened last night. Maybe get past all of this."

"I can meet you downstairs in the lobby in 15 minutes."

Briggs was there in seven minutes. She was too.

They left the dorm for a walk around campus. Discussion was awkward at first, both being careful about what they said. She asked about his bruise and whether it hurt.

"No problem. I'm sure his nose is hurting a lot more."

They both laughed. It broke the ice. They sat down on a bench. There was a fall chill in the air. Brenda wrapped her arms around herself keeping warm.

"Johnny. I know you didn't start that mess last night. He got what he deserved, and you gave it to him. I am just not used to being around violence like that. You are different than the boys that I have known in the past.

"They are college boys. When they've gone in the military, they are officers like Brandon, not corporals. They do not have tattoos. And, they certainly don't get into fistfights."

"What's with the tattoo thing? It's just a Marine Corps emblem. Pride in the Corps."

"The people I have seen with tattoos are merchant seamen and motorcycle gang members," she countered.

Briggs waited a few seconds before responding. "So, what does all that mean? I don't fit your image? I was thinking that what was more important was if we liked each other and enjoyed being together. We aren't discussing marriage here. I'm 300 miles away with at least another year left in the crotch."

"Don't call it the crotch. That's crude," Brenda said. Briggs knew he was walking on thin ice and needed to measure every word.

"What if we just try to put this behind us and keep seeing each other when we can," Brenda said. "Let's just see where it all goes. One day at a time."

"Or more accurately said, one weekend at a time," Briggs responded.

She kissed him. He kissed back. They hugged. They walked and talked. Things felt better. Two hours later he was headed back to Lejeune and he still had his girlfriend.

CHAPTER 11

November 1965
Camp Lejeune, North Carolina

Vietnam War Timeline: In the Ia Drang Valley, American troops fought their first large scale battle against the North Vietnamese Army. Both sides claimed victory. Nearly 300 Americans were killed. Their names are inscribed on Panel 3E of "The Wall."

Orders were coming in for the men who had come to the end of their two-year tour. Russell, Cross, Lindsay and Markham were all headed for Vietnam. They still had enough time left on their enlistments to serve the corps in another capacity and theater. No one knew what they would be doing on the other side of the pond, but all assumed it would be in a combat role.

Their friends left behind had mixed feelings. The lure of combat is an evil seductress. No one wants to go to war, but soldiers think of themselves as being bulletproof. It only happens to the other guy. If wounded, it will be a clean through and through in an arm or leg. Purple heart eligible with no lasting disabilities. They refuse to think about the possibility of getting their balls shot off.

Replacements were boots, recent graduates of the infantry training regiment, just across the New River at Camp Geiger, and one-year men fresh from radio school at Norfolk or San Diego.

It was up to recently promoted Gunnery Sergeant Ernie Lincoln to mold them into the unit, get them field trained and ready for deployment. Lincoln had just received his E-7 stripe, which meant a nice bump in pay and additional respect from the officers, senior NCOs and the ranks. It was the mark of a successful career.

Lincoln was counting on junior NCOs like Briggs and Gamboney to step up and show veteran leadership in the platoon. Gamboney got promoted to sergeant E-5 three weeks after joining the platoon.

Harold Parker, a squared away lance corporal who already was talking about re-enlisting when his initial contract was up in two years, would soon be promoted to corporal and was expected to take on additional responsibilities.

Military hierarchy is no different than civilian life. Kids join when they are 17, 18, 19 years old. They start at the bottom of the ladder. They are trained to follow orders and the system is built on them doing only what they are required to do. Nothing extra is expected or given.

Those who show extra ingenuity and willingness to work and stay out of trouble are rewarded with more rank, additional pay and benefits.

When first promoted, new NCOs are uneasy about supervising their buddies who they have been drinking and bitching with for the past year. Accepting the extra stripe means they have bought into the Mean Green Machine, the same as the lifers they often ridicule behind their back.

There can be some awkward moments when orders are given, received, resented and resisted. Briggs went through this with Mitchell and Jetland, who remained bad attitude PFCs long after they passed their normal promotion dates.

It does not take fresh NCOs long to buy into the deal. They like the improved lifestyle and more money in their pockets. The purchase of a car often followed shortly after promotion.

Briggs now did his drinking at the NCO club featuring a full liquor bar, table service, and restaurant style menu. It was a definite step up from socializing at the EM club which topped out with bottled beer and grocery store hot dogs under a heat lamp.

He could not go to their club. They were not welcome at his club. A divide developed in the old friendships. The system eventually wins out.

PFCs and lance corporals have no choice but to accept the new hierarchy. Replacement drinking buddies are easy to find.

The communications platoon command structure quickly took shape. Hotchkiss held weekly meetings to review the training schedule and goals with Lincoln, Gamboney, Briggs and Sergeant E-5 Tom Hamilton, who had transferred over from one of the line companies to head up the wire section.

Training had turned serious in the past few months. The battalion was constantly in the field leaving just enough time back in garrison to clean equipment, stand for inspections and get ready for the next assignment. Command post exercises, known as a CPX, were held monthly. This was practice for moving the commander, the staff and communications as battlefield conditions dictated.

It meant a lot of packing up tents, field tables and essential equipment then moving them multiple times to other locations while maintaining communications with aligned units. Comm platoon wiremen had to string new wire to guard posts. Three hours later they had to recover all the wire before moving again.

PFCs had to dig new fighting holes at each site and then fill them in before departing for the next location.

With simulated forces and a perceived enemy lurking somewhere in the bush, it all seemed like a lot of bullshit to the enlisted troops who did the physical labor. Officers viewed this as being a crucial component of playing war.

Lejeune's vast beaches, wetlands and piney woods offered plenty of space for movement. One exercise was even held in the Great Dismal Swamp on the North Carolina – Virginia border. The swamp lived up to its name raining non-stop for three days. The brass thought this environment best simulated what the Marines were facing in Vietnam.

A couple days of outdoor fun left Marines with an urge to scratch the numerous chigger bites they acquired. Chiggers are almost invisible to the naked eye. It requires a magnifying glass to spot them. The corpsmen carried a generic cream in their medical bags that minimizes the itching until the Marines were out of the field. The biggest fear were the bites in the groin area that caused something called summer penile syndrome, a swelling in a man's most valuable parts.

Briggs was named radio chief responsible for setting the daily watch schedules and radio equipment maintenance. He reported to the radio supervisor, Gamboney, who in turn reported to Gunnery Sergeant Lincoln, who reported to Lieutenant Hotchkiss. That was the chain of command.

Briggs watched his crew mature in the field. One of the crucial elements for success in battle is maintaining communication between units. Their performance was taken seriously, mistakes and failures noted and not forgotten.

The radios had to keep working and the radio operators, communicating both by voice and Morse Code, had to be competent at their jobs under all conditions. Radiomen working under a parka during a rainstorm in combat conditions needed to be as capable as a Navy signalman sitting in a ship's comfortable, well lighted operations center enjoying a cigarette and fresh cup of coffee.

The primary field radio was the AN/PRC-10, referred to as the Prick 10. It was introduced in 1951 during the Korean War. The Marines were always fighting the next war with equipment from the last war. The Prick 10 was a rugged radio designed to communicate with the Prick 6, better known as a walkie-talkie, and carried by fire team leaders. The problem was that the Prick 6 only seemed to work under ideal conditions.

Radio operators had to carry their own weapon and field equipment plus the Prick 10 which weighed 26 pounds with battery. Lugging extra batteries was a shared responsibility of the communication platoon.

Performance was judged seriously by all command levels up to the battalion commander, a lieutenant colonel, whose fitness report in this position was the most important he would have in his career.

He was only two ranks from becoming a general, which was the goal of every career officer. If his performance was deemed unsatisfactory by his superiors this was as high as he would go. A push into retirement would follow shortly.

An unmotivated teenaged radio operator not only could have a life and death impact on his fellow Marines during combat but also career implications for a field grade officer.

Even though Briggs considered PFC Danny Jetland to be a shit bird and troublemaker, in the field he was his best radio operator. Briggs had to learn to manage the good with the bad. He learned who he could rely on and who he could not.

Briggs and Gamboney worked well together as a management team. When they returned from the field, they would compare notes, review individual performances, set up new training schedules and altered assignments. A meeting with Lincoln and Hotchkiss followed.

During the previous three and half years of service, Briggs had never given any serious thought to making a career in the Marine Corps. But as he gained more responsibility and saw that he was good at it, the idea of becoming a sergeant was appealing.

He even began to investigate warrant officer programs and other career tracks. Becoming a commissioned officer still seemed to be a reach for him. However, as he recalled his evening with Army Lieutenant Brandon Hayes, he would entertain the thoughts that if Hayes could do it, why not him. Briggs felt that the only thing differentiating them were the brass bars on Hayes' collar.

CHAPTER 12

December 1965
Camp Lejeune, North Carolina

Vietnam War Timeline: Secretary of Defense Robert McNamara said that the number of U.S. troops in South Vietnam should be increased to 400,000 in 1966 and by an additional 200,000 in 1967. McNamara estimated that 1,000 Americans per month would die in the war and that "the odds are even" that the U.S. would prevail.

As the calendar creeped slowly towards the holidays the training schedule eased up which meant that the NCOs needed to find ways to keep the troops busy and out of trouble.

More time was spent in garrison cleaning communications and personal equipment. Field days in the barracks were frequent. What training the platoon did was held in the communications shack or in the adjacent vacant fields. Group calisthenics were held three days a week.

The dreaded "Junk on the Bunk" inspection was scheduled for mid-December. The penalty for not passing the inspection was the loss of holiday leave.

Daily work parties were formed each day and sent on what the troops considered bullshit assignments throughout Main Side Lejeune. Corporals were in charge meaning that Briggs was fully employed. Jobs included cleaning the garage at the motor pool, breaking down bunks in vacated barracks and doing a mattress inventory under the watchful eye of the notoriously cranky supply sergeant.

Winter in coastal North Carolina was relatively mild, but the temperatures occasionally dipped into the high 30s' with light snow flurries. Nothing stuck to the ground. The leaves dropped from the trees and grass turned brown. The barracks radiators began to crackle with heat as they were turned on for the first time since the previous March.

With 36 men sleeping in a barracks room, no one was happy with the temperature. In the middle of the night, a phantom in the comm platoon would silently sneak around and open all the windows. The sleeping Marines awoke at reveille to frigid temperatures. This caused an inordinate amount of bitching and grumbling and talk about what they would do if they were able to catch the secret window opener.

Standard issue field jackets never seemed to provide enough warmth to fight off the damp winter air. Most of the troops walked around with hunched shoulders and hands in their pockets, a violation of military protocol.

The Marines were checking out mentally, thinking about their holiday leaves. Half of the platoon got 10 days of Christmas leave beginning December 17 back on the 27th. The other half got their 10 days off over the New Year's holiday leaving when the others were returning. The unit would be at half strength for 20 days.

Briggs was sent to the field for two days to serve as a radio operator for a visiting captain from Marine Corps Schools Quantico who was assigned to judge a competition of field maneuvers by the various 8th Marines infantry companies.

The squads and fire teams practiced advancing on fortified positions, reacting to a gas attack, setting up and countering an ambush, creating a perimeter defense, determining fields of fire and conducting reconnaissance.

This was playing war without facing live enemy fire, which when added to the equation complicated real combat. Nevertheless, Briggs was impressed by the NCO leaders as they directed their squads. Practice, practice, practice would pay off in saving lives when they were in a real war.

Now that Vietnam was turning into a serious conflict, practice had a lot more meaning than it did before. Briggs made mental notes to himself as he listened to the captain's critiques of the exercises.

Briggs put in for leave with the second group over New Year's. He would spend Christmas on base and probably draw duty as NCO of the Day more than once. That was okay with him. Nothing much ever happened during this time of the year.

His first two years in the Marine Corps he did not take holiday leave. His first year he had just gotten back from boot leave and had reported into Communications & Electronics Battalion, San Diego, for training as a radio operator.

The next year, he was with 3/8 as they were deployed to the Caribbean, a standard three-month tour which kept a battalion of Marines at the ready in case of disruptions in that region.

After dropping off a company of Marines at Guantanamo Bay, Cuba, for fence line duty, the remainder of the battalion made a combat landing on the Puerto Rican island of Vieques, where they lived for a month training with naval gunfire, air support and infantry tactics.

The troops were allowed a few days of liberty in San Juan, then sailed to Panama for what was a planned week of jungle survival training under the supervision of Army instructors at Fort Sherman in the Panama Canal Zone.

On January 9, 1964, just one day after 3/8 landed for a week of jungle training, grievances between native Panamanians and "Zonians", or Americans residing within the U.S.-controlled Canal Zone, boiled over into a series of anti-American riots. That resulted in an evacuation of the U.S. embassy in Panama City, widespread looting, and some civilian deaths.

This period was later noted by historians as the beginning of the end of the U.S. controlled Canal Zone which was transferred to Panama in 1979.

As a show of American military presence, 3/8 spent the next two months living aboard ships docked at the Coco Solo Naval Base. The Marines trained on shore each day learning how to quell riots often in full view of Panamanians watching from the other side of a see-through fence.

Briggs had made it home to Battle Creek for Christmas in 1964. He wasn't sure what would happen this year now that Brenda was part of the plan. He was hoping they would be able to spend some additional time together.

He made another weekend trip to Fredericksburg during early December. This trip lacked the drama of the previous visit and that was okay with them. They avoided holiday sorority parties, sticking to themselves. They did drive to Washington and experienced the nightlife in Georgetown. They blended into the crowded streets with the under-30 generation listening to music in the crowded bars. They had a 50-mile drive back to Fredericksburg, so they were cautious about how much they had to drink.

Brenda stayed with him Saturday night at the Colonial. They watched TV. They talked. They cuddled. They kissed. They touched each other but that was as far as it went.

Briggs took Brenda to Goldy's for a drink. Goldy Harkness greeted Briggs like an old friend calling him Cassius. She even popped for the first round. It was not the sort of place that sorority girls from Mary Washington College would normally frequent. This was a walk on the wild side for her.

Before the weekend was over, they had discussed holiday plans. She invited him to spend New Year's at her home in Ardmore. This would be new territory for him, being on his best behavior, meeting her family.

As Lejeune emptied for Christmas those who were left felt they were on vacation. The officers who were not on leave would make a quick pass through the barracks each day to make sure everything was okay then they would disappear.

Gunnery Sergeant Lincoln did require the platoon to show up each morning at the comm shack where he would have some routine maintenance and training scheduled. He let them go after noon chow. Passes to leave the base were handed out like Christmas candy.

Everyone could feel the war in Vietnam heating up. Looking into the future no one knew who would and who would not be in the shit next Christmas.

CHAPTER 13

January 1966
Ardmore, Pennsylvania

Vietnam War Timeline: December 24, 1965 - President Lyndon Johnson announces a pause in Operation Rolling Thunder, the bombing of North Vietnam, while seeking peace negotiations. American war dead exceeded 2,300.

Briggs decided he would take just four days of holiday leave. He was not averse to making long drives in short periods. He was a Lejeune road warrior having made long weekend trips as far north as Boston and Miami to the south. He did not want to make the 900-mile drive home to Battle Creek now. If he got orders for Vietnam, he would want to use time then.

He left Camp Lejeune after morning chow on December 30, a Thursday. He drove to Brenda's house outside Philadelphia in just under eight hours. He planned to stay until Sunday, January 2nd. That was three overnights.

In accepting Brenda's invitation, he remembered his grandmother always said: "fish and guests stink after three days."

He was feeling plenty of anxiety about meeting her family, how he would fit in and how they would accept him. On New Year's Eve they were going to her father's country club for dinner. Having just been prepped at the sorority event on which fork to use and proper napkin etiquette, he felt he could handle this without embarrassing himself or Brenda. At least he was not going to have to wear his uniform. He spiffed up his civilian wardrobe borrowing a sport coat and a tie from one of his barracks buddies.

It was dark when he found the toney Chestnut Hill sub-division. Brenda had given him specific directions, but it was still confusing trying to navigate the winding streets and read addresses of the large homes sitting on half-acre lots. About four inches of snow covered the yards.

Briggs had grown up in a two-bedroom frame house with a side drive and a car port. From the looks of these homes his family house would have fit into an adjoining garage.

The neighborhood was intimidating. There was no turning back. He wondered if he would feel as much anxiety going into battle as he felt now.

The Kiley's home sat on a slight hill at the end of a long driveway which had recently been plowed. He was unsure if he should park his car there or in the street. He didn't want to look presumptuous, but he decided he would park in the driveway where he could make a fast getaway if this did not work out.

Brenda had been watching for him. She came out by herself to greet him. They did a quick kiss and hug, nothing too long in case they were being watched. He grabbed his overnight bag and a small box of Christmas presents for Brenda and her family that he had purchased at the PX where they had provided gift wrapping services.

On the drive to Pennsylvania Briggs had rehearsed his greetings with the family. Mother and father would be referred to as mister and missus unless permission was given to use first names. He did not expect that familiarity to be extended to him on his first visit.

Her father's professional name was P. Bartram Kiley, or Bart to friends, family and clients. It was certainly not to be used by his daughter's new boyfriend. What was his real first name? Presley. According to Brenda, it had been a perfectly good first name for her father, a tradition in every generation of the family, until Elvis Presley became famous. That is when he decided the P. would sound better professionally.

Mrs. Kiley was Ellen, not that he would call her that. Brenda's brother Shawn was a high school senior awaiting acceptance to one of the exclusive private New England colleges to which he applied such as Middlebury, Colby, and Bates. Brenda said her brother was smart and a good jock who planned to play lacrosse in college. Briggs knew nothing about lacrosse, it being more of an eastern sport. He figured any discussion of lacrosse and he would just keep his mouth shut. Mr. Kiley had already assumed that his son would follow his path through law school and into one of Philadelphia's Main Line firms.

Brenda led him into the house through the garage door which opened into a breezeway and then a modern, brightly lit and warm kitchen, a welcome change from the 20-degree cold outside. He smelled the juices of a rib roast simmering in the oven.

Mr. and Mrs. Kiley and Shawn were all standing in front of the fireplace in a large family room wearing brightly colored sweaters and looking like a Currier and Ives Christmas card. They all displayed unsure smiles curious to see what Corporal John Briggs, United States Marine Corps, was all about.

The introductions and handshakes went well along with the small talk like "how was your drive," and "did you have any problems finding the house."

Being military Briggs automatically worked "sir" and "ma'am" into every conversation. He had decided he would treat this visit as if he had been invited to the home of Camp Lejeune's commanding general, which of course, would never happen in real life.

Brenda had prepped him about the evening's schedule. Cocktails, a get-to- know you discussion around the fireplace followed by dinner.

"Can I get you something to drink," Mr. Kiley asked.

Mr. Kiley was drinking something brown with ice cubes. Briggs figured it was scotch or bourbon that had come out of a fancy looking cut glass decanter that was sitting in an alcove with other similar bottles. Mrs. Kiley was drinking wine.

After the long drive, Briggs really wanted to have a beer. Brenda took care of that issue. She knew what he wanted and handed him an open bottle of Heineken, with a glass half poured.

"Dad, Marines like a beer after a long drive," she explained. This girl was a winner.

The small talk went well as Briggs relaxed and felt he hit the right notes with the family asking them enough questions to balance the discussion and avoid being on the hot seat. Afterall, Mr. Kiley was an attorney and presumably skilled at cross examination.

Brenda showed small signs of affection holding his hand while they sat on the couch together. She pitched in with college life stories that took the spotlight off Briggs.

Her parents were tactful without being rude at extracting information from Briggs about his family's life in Battle Creek. There was no question the Briggs family lived in a different economic class than the Kiley family. He had no intention of trying to make things look different than what they were, not that he could. His family was hard working, lower middle class who paid their taxes on time and did not commit crimes. What else did he need to say?

Because of the fame of the Kellogg company and the power of their television advertising, Battle Creek was a better-known city than most of its size. The Kiley family showed an interest and wanted to know what it was like for Briggs' parents to be employees of the most famous cereal company in the world.

After they sat down to dinner the discussion turned to the expanding war in Vietnam. Newspapers and television were now reporting daily on the clash of opinions among segments of the American public and government. College campuses were becoming the scene of frequent confrontations and occasional violence. Troop deployments were increasing. Reported body counts on both sides were causing distress.

Mary Washington College was not a hotbed of radicalism, but students across the nation were drawing battle lines between themselves and their parents' generation. Brenda and Briggs, in their relatively short dating life, had avoided deep discussions of the topic.

It did not take long for Bart and Ellen Kiley to make their opinions known. Surprisingly, they seemed to be on different sides of the issue. Even more surprising to Briggs was that Ellen seemed to be the hawk in the family while Bart was the dove. Briggs noted there was some sharpness between them as the discussion evolved.

Even though he had never seen or heard a shot fired in anger, Briggs knew they would expect him to have an opinion. Brenda rescued him by suggesting a change of subject.

The remainder of the evening was spent discussing sports, movies, the post-holiday travel plans of the Kiley family and Shawn's college options. Brenda suggested that she and Briggs take a brisk winter walk to see the neighborhood Christmas decorations.

"I thought it was time for us to get out of there for a while," she confessed. "You had enough of the third-degree interrogation."

By the time they got home Bart was having a late-night drink and was reading a book that Briggs thought was large enough to be used as a door stop. It was a history of Europe's dark ages he briefly explained. No additional inquiry was necessary. Ellen had gone up to bed and Shawn was nowhere to be found.

Brenda directed Briggs to the guest room. She made sure he had enough blankets and clean towels. They exchanged a good night kiss.

"You did good tonight Marine," she whispered. "I'm so glad you came. They liked you. See you in the morning. Sleep as late as you want. We don't sound reveille around here."

The next morning Mr. Kiley invited Briggs to ride with him to his office. "Just going in to check the mail and pick up a couple of files to review over the weekend. It will give us some time to talk," he commented.

Briggs did not know how to say no, and when Brenda gave him a slight nod of her head, he figured he should accept the invite.

As Mr. Kiley drove the car, he asked Briggs about Marine Corps life, what he thought of Vietnam, would he have to go overseas and what were his plans after his enlistment ended.

Briggs knew he was being interrogated. He kept his answers somewhat vague, not because he was trying to avoid anything, but he was not sure himself what he thought about Vietnam and his future.

"I never served. Always felt a bit incomplete that I didn't," Mr. Kiley said. "I wish I had. My time came after World War Two and before Korea. They were dismantling the Army in those days. You couldn't get into the military even if you begged them.

"Korea came along. That wasn't exactly a shining period in American history. I know you can't choose your war but that one wasn't good for anyone. I hope Vietnam works out better for us, and you, if you have to go."

Briggs felt a connection forming between the two men. Mr. Kiley talked about his career and his hopes that Brenda might also follow his path to law school. "There are so many more women lawyers now. I could see her doing well," he argued.

Briggs picked up what he thought was a subliminal message being sent his way, such as: "don't get in the way of my daughter's future."

The remainder of the visit proceeded without any major drama other than Ellen Kiley getting tipsy at the country club dinner. As soon as they arrived she immediately began working the room flitting from table to table. Briggs was wondering if she was running for office. People were constantly stopping at their table to say hello and offer seasonal greetings. Ellen seemed to be the main social attraction. Turns out she was being nominated for club vice-president at the next election.

As Ellen was relating a story to her family about club politics, she got animated and knocked over her wine glass. Waiters rushed to the rescue doing a quick tablecloth change. An embarrassed silence ensued over the Kiley table as Ellen apologized slurring her words. Briggs was happy it was her and not him that got drunk.

Briggs left Sunday morning, three days after arrival just about the same time that fish would begin to stink. He and Brenda spent a few minutes alone before he hit the road. Their goodbye was warm and cuddly making plans for their next visit as soon as she was back in school. Bart and Shawn offered handshakes and Mrs. Kiley gave him a hug and the usual goodbye well wishes. Briggs left feeling that the trip had been a success.

CHAPTER 14

February 1966
Camp Lejeune, North Carolina

Vietnam Timeline: American military strength in Vietnam was 184,314, compared to 23,300 the year before. "Operation Masher," the largest search and destroy mission of the war, was launched. The name was later changed to "Operation White Wing," because Masher was deemed too crude by the White House.

Winter weather in coastal North Carolina is a mixture of dreary, gray, dampness with periodic wet snow that turns into slush after a few hours. Occasionally there is a day of sunshine and temperatures that reach into the high 50's.

The uncertainty of the war buildup, who is going and who is staying, dominated the Lejeune and Jacksonville community. Career officers and staff NCOs figured this was their chance to go to war and further their career. Families began to make plans for when husbands and fathers got their orders.

Marines below the rank of corporal, the guys who do the actual fighting, had mixed feelings. Most of them were only committed to serve one enlistment. They were looking at four years and out and the rest of their lives to call themselves ex-Marines, not dead Marines. They weren't thinking about their careers. It was more a matter of "will I get out of the crotch before they send me over?"

There was a lot of bitterness over the automatic enlistment extensions that were announced the previous August. In many cases, the extra four months tacked onto the end of active duty contracts was just enough time to qualify for a Vietnam assignment. Every unit seemed to have one man whose enlistment was scheduled to end one day after the extension went into effect.

The Marine full tour of duty was 13 months, but with the need to build up the force quickly men with valuable skill sets, like radio operators, were getting orders with as little as nine months left on their enlistments.

Briggs was not sure about his future. The time left on his enlistment with the extension, was right at the minimum cutoff. If he did not get orders in the next month or two, it was likely he would serve out the rest of his time at Lejeune and get discharged. The relationship with Brenda had become a factor in his decision making.

He liked serving in the Marine Corps but the idea of being a lifer was not that enticing. His view of career NCOs was that of a life challenged by serving a higher mistress who accepted no excuses for not being where she wanted you regardless of how much personal pain that caused your family.

It seemed to him that many senior NCOs that were not married spent as much time as they could drinking at the NCO club. In general, they were a lonely group who were needed in the Marine Corps for their professional knowledge and experience but whose personal lives bordered on being pathetic.

Those who had families lived off base in substandard housing, drove crappy cars and were always challenged by not having enough money to support their wife and kids.

There is an old saying that "if the Marine Corps wanted you to have a wife, they would have issued you one."

The next promotion was never enough. The goal was to stick it out for 20 years to get the military retirement benefits, which look good when you are 18, but not so good when you are 38 and need to find a new career. A resume highlighting your skills at being a good machine gunner does not help you find a job in the civilian world.

If Briggs wanted to become an officer, he would have to leave active duty for a few years, get a college degree and come back in through Officer Candidate School. The "mustang" path that made overnight officers during World War Two and Korea had been phased out years before. The few mustangs left in the Marine Corps were viewed as dinosaurs who were rarely promoted above the rank of major.

Life in 3/8 was back to the basics, daily training schedules that alternated between equipment maintenance, occasional field exercises, physical fitness and inspections. Monday through Friday, the communications platoon was required to maintain a radio net 24/7 with units conducting exercises in the camp's vast training areas.

As Radio Chief, Briggs set up the rotation and training schedules, supervised equipment maintenance and was the first call when anything went wrong. Briggs had to make himself available whenever a radio net was operating. if he handled the job well it was the road to earning the stripe of a sergeant E-5.

Each Monday morning, he was included in the meeting with Lieutenant Hotchkiss, Gunny Lincoln, Gamboney, and the other NCOs to discuss the week's schedule. He was involved in personnel reviews and was expected to speak honestly about performance and abilities – the good and the bad, including those who were his friends.

Corporals were pulled in two directions, enjoying the benefits and responsibilities of being an NCO, while feeling a loyalty to their buddies who had not yet been promoted. This was the rank where personal decisions had to be made about moving up ...or out.

Since the holiday visit with Brenda's family, Briggs had only missed one weekend in Fredericksburg. She had exams coming and needed the time to study, so he stayed on base and traded with another corporal serving as duty NCO. This way he was owed a favor later when he would need it.

The weekend hotel visits had put a crimp on his budget, so Brenda found him a place to stay with the brother of one of her classmates in a dumpy rental house a few blocks from campus with two other guys. Briggs had to sleep on a couch but that didn't matter to him. He reciprocated when he showed up with a case of beer. That kept him on good terms with his roommates and was more in line with his budget.

Their relationship had reached a new level when they finally decided to have sex. Neither one of them were overly experienced. Briggs was quite sure Brenda was a virgin but was not about to ask nor did it matter.

He'd had a short-lived relationship with a high school classmate in Battle Creek that primarily consisted of some clumsy groping, petting and the use of a condom in the back seat of his father's '54 Ford.

His only other experience involved a San Juan bar girl when the battalion pulled liberty there during its Caribbean tour of duty the previous year. He considered that part of his personal history best forgotten.

Brenda turned 22 on February 9th. To celebrate, they splurged on a nice dinner at an Italian restaurant followed by the privacy of a room at the Colonial Motor Lodge. They split the costs. It was her idea.

Their weekends together now increasingly included a search for some space and time alone. Twice he had the rental house to himself when his roommates were gone.

It was Brenda's idea to visit Briggs at Camp Lejeune. She had never been to a military base before and was curious. Briggs had anxiety about her visit but didn't push back too hard. He was pleased that she wanted to know more about his life. Brenda was able to get a ride with a sorority sister who was making a weekend trip to see her family in Wilmington just 50 miles south of Jacksonville.

Briggs booked a room for $14 a night at the on-base Hospitality House Hotel, known by the acronym of Ho Ho. The rooms were small but adequate with a double bed and television over the bureau. This was like being on a vacation together.

"This place reminds me of a huge college campus," she commented after he gave her the obligatory tour of the base. She was impressed with its pristine appearance and the colonial architecture of the command buildings.

They went to the movies at the base theater, attended a performance by Frank Sinatra, Jr., who was making the rounds of military camps, and had dinner at the NCO club which featured a musical group playing all Motown hits.

They spent two hours on Sunday afternoon wandering around the PX. "Everything is so cheap. I could get in some big trouble here," Brenda commented. Using Briggs' military ID card, she bought herself a new wristwatch. He wanted to buy it for her, but she refused to let him.

They had spent a weekend as young lovers enjoying each other and ignoring the realities of the world around them. She knew but preferred not to dwell on the camp's real purpose, to train warriors who may eventually pay the ultimate price in war.

As Briggs drove her off-base late Sunday afternoon to meet her ride back to Fredericksburg, the tackiness of a military town sank in. She had arrived after dark on Friday and being anxious to see him, she had not paid much attention to her surroundings.

Now she saw the seemingly endless used car lots, pawn shops, tattoo parlors, liquor stores, strip bars and cheap motels that lined both sides of Lejeune Boulevard between the base main gate and downtown Jacksonville.

Brenda's ride was waiting for her at a rest area on Highway 17 just outside town. She and Briggs did a long kiss and hug. Goodbyes got longer and tougher each weekend.

CHAPTER 15

March 1966
Camp Lejeune, North Carolina

Vietnam War Dateline: The NVA won a strategic but costly victory at the Battle of A Shau Valley over a greatly outnumbered force of American Special Forces and their Vietnamese allies. The Green Berets suffered a one hundred percent casualty rate while holding off the NVA for two days.

"Corporal Briggs. Front and Center." Gunny Lincoln shouted from his office in the back of the comm shack. It was a boot camp type command that was rarely used in the Fleet Marine Force. Lincoln liked to employ his drill field voice occasionally just to reemphasize to the troops that this was a top down autocratic military organization.

Briggs laughed knowing that the gunny was just exercising his lungs but decided to give him an appropriate boot camp type response.

In a loud voice while snapping to attention Briggs stepped in front of Lincoln's desk: "Sir, Corporal Briggs reporting as ordered, Sir!"

"Don't call me sir, shithead. I'm not one of those pussy officers. Close the door and take a seat." Lincoln enjoyed the roll play. He liked Briggs, trusting him more than any of the other junior NCOs in the platoon, often assigning him tasks above his pay grade knowing the job would get done the way he expected.

Similarly, Briggs enjoyed working for Lincoln. They had developed a mentor and student relationship. The gunny didn't put up with any shit but was fair with the men. Briggs thought Lincoln's professional knowledge was almost legendary. He had witnessed Lincoln time again coax life into the seemingly temperamental radios when they would go on the blink or atmospheric conditions blocked connections.

Lieutenant Hotchkiss too valued Gunny Lincoln like a head football coach values a coordinator, letting him call the plays and run the offense. Life is easier for a young Marine officer with an experienced senior NCO who can manage the outfit.

"The L-T says we have five overseas billets to fill from the platoon. Only people with at least 13 months left on their enlistments can go. In other words, enough time to spend a full tour killing gooks.

"According to your personnel file, even with the extension, you've only got 7 months left before we kick your ass out on the streets. Re-enlist, or extend your enlistment."

There was an awkward silence as Briggs processed what was being presented to him.

"Well? What are you thinking?" Lincoln broke the silence. He cocked his head in anticipation of an answer.

"Was that supposed to be my shipping over speech, Gunny? If it is, you sort of suck at the salesmanship part."

"Yeah, that's one reason they never sent me to recruiter school. So, I'm checking to see where your head is at. Briggs, you are a good Marine. The crotch can use you over there."

"And, what's in it for me?"

"Did I mention that you could get another stripe if you went over?"

"Whoopee. Big deal. I get $75 more a month at least until I get my ass shot off. I don't know Gunny, so far, I don't see many high points in this. I have this serious girlfriend now. She is looking forward to me getting out. Starting a life together."

"Yeah. I see guys get out all the time thinking the grass is always greener. You become a raggedy assed civilian. Get all caught up with the little lady, having to bring home a paycheck from some shit ass factory job, and before long you're wishing you were back in the crotch."

"Gee, I hadn't thought about it that way," Briggs said sarcastically. "You sure are a sweet talker Gunny."

They both laughed at the interchange. Briggs did not like to admit it to his buddies, but he liked serving in the Marine Corps. If he told any of them, they would call him a lifer. Since the festivities had begun in 'Nam he had spent more time than he would admit thinking about being there. This is what all the Marine Corps indoctrination and training was designed to do, turn them into warriors. No one ever thought bad things were going to happen to them. It was always the other guy who got his nuts shot off.

Gunny Lincoln let it slip that he was planning on putting in for one of the overseas billets. He figured he had to go eventually. Might as well get on board early. Having served in Korea the gunny was no virgin to combat. He had looked down the wrong side of a rifle barrel before. Going to war was his destiny.

Briggs did not say no. He did not say yes. He said he would think about it. Lincoln told him he had three days to decide before he needed to fill the billets. He would ask for volunteers. If he did not get enough, well then, somebody would be pissed when he learned he drew the short straw.

Gamboney was the Vietnam veteran Briggs knew best. They had connected sharing a few beers at the NCO club and having bunks next to each other. Briggs considered him to be a solid guy as he watched Gamboney gain the respect of the troops, Gunny Lincoln and the LT.

"Hey Rich. You got time for a beer tonight? I'll buy the first round."

"Big deal. That just means I have to buy the second round," Gamboney responded. "Let's do it. My social calendar is light."

The club alternatively featured specials on the cheapest beers available – Falstaff and Carling Black Label being the two most popular.

"The gunny is encouraging me to extend six months to go to 'Nam. What do you think about that?"

"I'm not going to tell you what to do and then after you get all fucked up you'll come back here and kill me. This is a decision you need to make on your own."

"Yeah. I know that. This would not be on you. It's on me. I'm just looking for some insight. I haven't decided if I want to stay in the green machine or get the fuck out. I have this girlfriend now and things are going well there. On the other hand, I'm bored to death sitting around Lejeune. That would be my life for the next 7 months until I get out.

"Then I don't know what I'm going to do when I get out. Go back to Michigan? Go to college? Get a job? It's not like I feel any special calling."

"What's the girl thinking?" Gamboney asked.

"That's a good question. She graduates from college in a few months. I am not sure about her plans. She has talked about going to law school. Her old man is a hot shot lawyer in Philadelphia. I suppose she might go in that direction. Not sure how I would fit into her picture.

"I see other guys heading over the big pond and I feel like I should be with them. There is my family to think about also. If I told my mother I volunteered to go she would freak out."

"Yeah. I got you. That's like an automatic reaction by mothers," Gamboney responded. They both sat quietly for a few minutes drinking their beers.

"I've gone through the same thought process as you. Nothing in the civilian world appeals to me all that much. I am good at this job. I have decided to stay with it. If this Vietnam thing lasts, I will end up going back. I'm alright with that even though next time I might not be so lucky."

Gamboney spun his stool around so he was facing Briggs. "John, you're good at this job. I've watched you. The troops respect you. They do the things you tell them to do because they want to do it for you. That's not something that comes easy to everyone. You have natural leadership skills.

"I've served with a lot of shit NCOs, and officers. We can't change all the bad things about the Marine Corps, but we can make a difference in our own little corner of the world.

"The medals and stripes don't mean shit, but we might keep some kid from getting killed someday. They need us over there. In my way of thinking, we might not get paid as much, but this job is a hell of a lot more important than being a lineman for the phone company. I guess that means something to me. I may regret it someday, but for now paint me green and call me gung ho."

They finished off four beers each and a cheeseburger. Gamboney described life in Vietnam, living each day with the risk of getting blown up, trudging through rice paddies looking for Charlie. It sounded like a typical Marine Corps cluster fuck. To a civilian it would mean run as fast as you could in the opposite direction.

To Briggs it just whetted his appetite. This was why he went in the Marine Corps. He knew what he had signed up for. When he left the club that night, he knew what his decision would be.

CHAPTER 16

March 1966
Fredericksburg, Virginia

Vietnam War Timeline: "The Ballad of the Green Berets" by Staff Sergeant Barry Sadler, a Special Forces Medic, became a major hit reaching #1 on the Billboard Hot 100. It inspired a wave of patriotism in the U.S.

Briggs extended his enlistment one year. His new discharge date was July 1967. He would then have to make another decision at that time about whether to stay in the Marine Corps or not. He was sure his mind would be clearer after a Vietnam tour of duty.

He signed his papers on a Wednesday morning. The battalion S-1 (Personnel) C.O. was Major Ralph Whitehead. He and Briggs knew each other from their time together in H&S Company when Whitehead was still a captain and had been the company commander. Briggs thought he was one of the better officers he had served with in the Marine Corps.

"You sure you want to do this lad? You're taking a big step. If you sit tight, you can just stay here for another seven months and then you can go home. Your obligation to the Big Green Machine will be all done," Whitehead said.

"Yes sir. I understand. Thanks for the advice. I'm pretty set on what I want to do."

As he attached his signature both to the enlistment extension and to his transfer orders, he could feel Whitehead's words adding to his nagging doubt. No one with a clear mind voluntarily signs up to go to war. He knew this could be a life or death decision.

He had two weeks to report to Camp Pendleton, California, where he would spend a month in advanced infantry training before heading to Vietnam.

Briggs requested ten days of leave which would allow him to spend a weekend with Brenda, then drive home to Michigan to try and explain to his parents why he did what he did. He would leave his car with is family in Battle Creek and use the rest of his travel pay on an airplane trip to San Diego.

Briggs had not discussed his decision in advance with Brenda or anyone in his family. He knew this was going to be a shock to them all. No one other than his Marine buddies would understand.

It was a Friday when Briggs left Lejeune for the last time after morning chow with all his belongings packed into the tiny trunk and back seat of his blue Volkswagen bug. Having lived out of a footlocker and half a wall locker for the past two years, he did not own all that much other than his uniforms and some cheap civvies.

The goodbyes with his buddies were brief. People are constantly coming and going in the Marine Corps. No one spends a lot of time on farewells. There is some exchanging of home addresses with the guys who were getting out soon. Others just assumed they would be following to Vietnam.

"Stay in touch buddy. Keep your head down. I'll see you across the pond," Mitchell told him.

He had told Brenda he would be in Fredericksburg earlier than usual but had not explained why. Part of his government travel expense allocation would pay for a room at the Colonial Motor Lodge for two nights.

Her last class ended at 2 p.m. Briggs had called her earlier in the week from the pay phone behind the mess hall to let her know that he would be there no later than 3 p.m. He did not explain his agenda and she did not ask. Calls from pay phones were kept under three minutes so details are left for when you did not have to add two more quarters to keep the line alive.

Briggs felt like his car knew the way without him. Leave the main gate behind, turn left on Lejeune Boulevard towards Jacksonville, connect to North Carolina Route 24 to Kinston 40 miles away. That is where he would take the shortcut that no longer seemed so short through Snow Hill to Wilson. All two-lane highways.

He connected with I-95 outside Wilson. This is where he made up time. He passed the familiar exits at Rocky Mount, Roanoke Rapids, Emporia, Petersburg and Richmond.

Other than the anticipation he always felt at seeing Brenda, this was not a drive he would miss. He rode in silence. No radio. No music. His mind was on what and how he would tell Brenda that he was headed overseas. What impact would this have on their relationship he was not sure.

After telling Brenda he would then have to figure out how to deal with his family. He could work on that during the 10-hour drive to Battle Creek. One thing at a time.

He checked into the Colonial. Lucy, the daytime desk clerk greeted him warmly. "How you doing Corporal Briggs? Glad to see you back with us again."

Briggs liked being treated as a regular customer. He would miss their weekends snuggled in the big double bed at the Colonial watching TV while eating pizza. He unloaded his belongings from the back of the car putting them in the hotel storage area that Lucy had opened for him. He was going over to meet Brenda. A packed car would raise immediate questions that he was not ready to answer.

Brenda was waiting for him in the residence hall lobby. They hugged and kissed. Neither one of them were comfortable with over the top displays of public affection but they held each other longer than usual. She threw in a low moan and a smile as wide as the Rappahannock River that melted him.

"I've really missed you. You have a lot of making up to do this weekend Marine." They had not seen each other since she visited Camp Lejeune three weeks before. Briggs had to stay on base one weekend for a field exercise and the next week she had to go home to Philadelphia for a family wedding.

Spring had arrived in northern Virginia. Temperatures were in the high 60s, trees and flowers were blooming. They drove to a rustic park about 20 miles away with a picturesque overlook of the Potomac. They walked the trails hand in hand down to the riverbank where they dipped their feet in the water.

He updated her on the past couple of weeks activity at Lejeune while she described the wedding and her time with her family. Each time they were together they talked more about their life before they met, getting to know each other better. Any discussion of the future was colored in gray tones left for another time. The present was all that mattered. They had become a couple, totally comfortable with each other in conversation, desires and physical needs.

After they got back to town, they stopped at Goldy's for a beer and a hamburger. Goldy treated them like old friends. It being a Friday night Sergeant Fee and his buddies were celebrating the end of the week's shift.

"Hey Corporal Briggs, you're staying out of trouble these days, right? No messing up my town. Make sure you check your guns at the city limit." He sat down with them to shoot the shit as Marine Corps slang would describe it.

Fee wanted to know about the war and what was happening at Lejeune. He had kept in touch with two of his buddies who had stayed in the Marine Corps after his discharge. One of them had gone to 'Nam and was killed by a booby trap during a search and destroy mission late in '65. Fee was obviously saddened by the loss of his friend.

"I hope they can get this shit cleared up over there before too many people get hurt. It seems to me to be a bit of a mess. We've got the hardliners on one side that want to go kick gook ass and then we've got all these college kids and hippies protesting and causing trouble all over the country." He looked at Brenda with a quizzical expression. She stayed silent on the matter.

Briggs was relieved that Fee did not ask him about whether he would be going overseas. He didn't want that conversation to begin before he was ready. Fee had downed more than a couple of beers. He wanted to talk more than listen. Fee dominated the conversation until he decided it was time for him to go home. As he left, he threw twenty bucks on the table. "Tonight, is on me kids. See you next time you're in town."

Briggs thought to himself, "If I'm ever back in town."

They spent the night in each other's arms. They were no longer inexperienced and tentative lovers. They now expressed their passion without embarrassment or caution.

On Saturday, Brenda had to spend a few hours studying for an upcoming exam. They spent the afternoon at the college library. While she hit the books, Briggs read magazines and newspapers sitting in one of the big easy chairs next to the sunlit floor to ceiling windows. He had always been a reader so spending a day in a library was a treat.

Afterwards, they went back to Goldy's for a beer. A couple of Brenda's friends joined them. Goldy's was not a usual college hangout but Goldy welcomed them from behind the bar, making sure to check their IDs. Briggs and Brenda had previously been vetted. The three women talked about college and classes and their friends. That was okay with Briggs. He did a good job of acting interested in their stories, but with time passing, his mind was on something else more important.

After dinner at a Chinese restaurant they were back in Room 247 at the Colonial Motor Lodge laying together on the bed when Briggs decided it was time: "There's something I need to talk to you about." His tone of voice was serious and somber.

He waited for her to respond or at least to look at him. She did neither. She stared at the wall.

"I'm headed to Vietnam."

She still did not speak.

"We aren't going to see each other again for more than a year."

When she still didn't speak, Briggs said: "Do you have anything you want to say? Anything you want to ask me?"

She took a couple of deep breaths and finally looked at him. Tears were forming in her eyes.

"I knew it. I knew something was up since you got here. You were holding back all weekend. I thought you didn't have to go. You don't have enough time left in your enlistment."

"Yeah. That's right. I extended."

"You mean nobody made you do it? You just up and decided one day that they couldn't fight a war without you. Right? The big fucking hero. Now you're going over there and who knows if you'll ever come back."

Briggs was more surprised at her use of the word "fucking" than he was of her apparent anger. He had never heard her use that word before.

"I know you don't understand. It's just something I have to do."

"No. I don't fucking understand. Nobody would understand. What about your parents? Have you told them yet?"

"No. Not yet. I'm headed home tomorrow to tell them."

"So, is this it? You are just gone, and I don't see you again? What have I been to you, just the flavor of the month? Do you have a girl in every port? Love 'em and leave 'em? We couldn't have discussed this first?"

"It's not like that."

"Yeah, it is like that. Now I am supposed to sit around like a war bride writing love letters and waiting for my big hero to return from the crusades.

"We're not engaged. We never talked about being in love or getting married. You do not have any obligation to me. I know all that. But I did think we were in a relationship. I thought you were my boyfriend not my pen pal.

"Oh, and thanks for giving me so much lead time on this new plan of yours. The night before you leave for a year. I'm surprised you didn't just send me a postcard from Danang."

"Brenda. I do love you. I don't want to lose you. But this is something I have to do."

"Well, I'm sorry but I don't share your passion for combat. I can't understand how or why you could have done this?"

She put on her coat, grabbed her purse and walked out the door.

"Where are you going," Briggs shouted. "Wait. Please."

"When you get where you're going, drop me a line sailor boy."

Those were the last words they spoke.

PART II

*"The ultimate outcome of a war is not always to
be regarded as final."*
(Carl von Clausewitz)

CHAPTER 17

April 1966
Danang, Republic of Vietnam

Vietnam War Timeline: A Buddhist uprising in I Corps created an armed confrontation between a platoon of U.S. Marines who blocked the passage of a convoy of ARVN soldiers from a takeover of Danang Air Base. Previous unrest had resulted in Buddhist monks burning themselves to death in public.

The flight from Okinawa to Vietnam took six hours. The C-130 Hercules turboprop was not designed with passenger comfort in mind. It was meant to carry cargo and to drop paratroopers off the back ramp. Canvas seating without back support was available along the bulkheads and one strip down the center of the fuselage. A single toilet was available behind a canvas partition. There was little sound protection from the giant engines. It was just a flying boxcar.

When his lower back began to stiffen up over the South China Sea, Briggs unbuckled his seat belt and found a spot to lay down on a pile of life jackets. The plane did not encounter any significant turbulence, so he was able to ride out the rest of the trip in relative comfort.

When the plane began its descent into Danang, the 80 Marines aboard could feel the air temperature heat up along with their anxiety levels. One of the flight crew reported that the weather upon landing was sunny with a high of 102 degrees. There was no mention of suffocating humidity that they would all come to know too well.

There were only a couple portholes on each side of the plane so no one could see out. They could only guess where they were and how high until the wheels bounced on the runway. The C-130 was not made for smooth landings. It was built for operating on unprepared air strips.

It took about ten minutes to taxi to a stop. Having been immobile for the duration of the flight, getting legs moving and stretching out the back was the first challenge. Everyone grabbed their gear and lined up to debark. They had been allowed to bring one sea bag with just the essentials, that being three sets of utility uniforms, changes of underwear, and some personal items. No dress uniforms were necessary. They were going to war.

The remainder of their belongings had been left in a second sea bag stored in a warehouse in Okinawa to hopefully be recovered 13 months later.

Briggs and the other men had flown to Okinawa the previous week in a C-141 Star Lifter, the military's version of a passenger jet. It left from Marine Corps Air Station El Toro, south of Los Angeles on a Wednesday afternoon. It made one refuel stop in the middle of the night on Wake Island, crossed the International Date Line and landed at Kadena Air Base Friday morning. The trip took 18 hours, but two days had passed. It was a day lost that could only be recaptured on their return to the U.S.

As they filed off the plane in Vietnam the bright sunlight, heat, humidity and the smell of jet fuel rocked their senses. A refueling truck had already attached itself to the plane getting it ready for a return flight. It was on a commuter run ferrying troops back and forth to the U.S. military bases in southeast Asia.

A company of Marines wearing tattered looking utility uniforms and relieved smiles stood in formation waiting to head home. The departing salts couldn't resist the opportunity to shout derisive comments at the new arrivals.

"You'll be sorry!"

"Enjoy the Nam."

"See you in a year, boys."

Condescending laughs followed. An NCO told them to shut up.

Busses were waiting to take Briggs and the others to a processing center on the west side of the base. They piled on with their sea bags. Open windows provided no relief from the heat. The green foliage of Hill 327, five klicks to the west, and Monkey Mountain, 20 klicks to the east, loomed over the base.

Ten minutes later they were standing outside a Quonset hut where they were met by Lance Corporal Jackman, clerk / typist, who told them to hand over their military record envelopes which they had carried with them from California.

Besides the PFCs and lance corporals who were most of the group, there were also two majors, a captain and a couple lieutenants, five senior NCOs, and three corporals including Briggs. Each rank hung with their own. Jackman treated all ranks the same. His job was to get them through as quickly as possible. He wasn't trying to make friends.

"It's going to be a couple hours at least before we process all your assignments, so make yourself comfortable and don't go too far away." He said it in that pissed off way that all clerks and cooks seemed to share. They were not combat Marines unless you counted a typewriter or a frying pan as their weapon. They felt they had got the short end of the stick when military occupations were assigned.

Even though they had crappy attitudes, no one gave clerks any grief because they could make the decision where you ended up: a plush headquarters assignment or as a line company grunt.

Finding comfort was a major challenge since there was limited shade and the only place to sit was on a sea bag. They spread out on the available ground and did what Marines are good at doing: "hurry up and wait."

The only thing to keep them busy was to watch the flight operations on the adjoining runways. Jet fighters, helicopters, transport planes and all sorts of military aircraft were landing and taking off one after another.

Briggs had spent a year at 3/8 assigned to the Forward Air Control Team, including three weeks of special training at Little Creek Naval

Base in Virginia. He was especially interested in watching the A-4 Sky-hawk jets. It was the primary attack plane used by the Navy and the Marine Corps. They meant serious business. Briggs imagined the damage and destruction the planes had created as they returned from their missions.

Marine Corps friendships are forged and forgotten quickly. Nobody got too close because relationships were sure to end due to transfers, discharges or during a war in more sudden and tragic ways.

Lieutenants talk to lieutenants. Sergeants talk to sergeants. Corporals talk to corporals. During training in California Briggs had connected with Corporal Bob Sneed, from Charleston, South Carolina. They had pulled a couple of liberties together during their pre-Vietnam training at Camp Pendleton. Sneed had an Administrative MOS so Briggs thought he would know what was happening behind the scenes.

"What happens now?" Briggs asked.

"They'll probably go to lunch and leave us sitting out here roasting in the fucking sun," Sneed answered as he wiped his dust covered face. "I figure there's some pissed off captain or major in there throwing darts at a board to decide who goes where. Don't expect any favors."

"Why is it that all captains and majors seem to be permanently pissed off?" Briggs said. It was a rhetorical question.

"Yeah. They're all lifers fucking each other for the next rank or assignment. They're probably loving this war shit. Most of them want to leave here with a purple heart and at least a bronze star on their record."

They had been awake since 0300. It was now pushing 1500 hours. They had been fed a box lunch on the plane consisting of a sandwich made with thick white bread and a couple slices of meat that was impossible to identify, an apple and bag of chips.

After two hours clerk typist Lance Corporal Jackman began to reappear with a few personnel jackets at a time calling out names with assignments.

"Lipman, Ward, Horwitz, Fish. 3/9. Your ride will be here in about an hour. Hang close by. They'll pick you up here." He handed the envelopes back to each Marine.

Ten minutes later he was back again. "Cotter and Ayers." They stood up to make themselves known. "First Shore Party Battalion. Your unit is up at Phu Bai. You got a plane ride ahead of you. Go down to the Transport Unit, it's about three huts down and give them your orders. They'll figure how to get you up there."

Those with assignments shook hands with their buddies wishing each other well. Everyone was standing now waiting for Jackman to announce their futures. It was obvious that all the assignments had been made as he disappeared into the Quonset hut long enough to grab a new pile of unit assignments.

"Russell, Donohue, Scanlon and...let's see, I got two Smiths – Robert K. and B.O. Smith. You're all headed to 1/7. They're down in Chu Lai but I am told they got some transport up here on the base and should be cruising by shortly so don't disappear. You've got a nice truck ride ahead of you. Keep your heads down."

Jackman was playing God with other people's lives. He thought he was being funny. No one appreciated his sense of humor. This was like waiting around to see who made the varsity basketball team only with more significant implications.

Phu Bai and Chu Lai were about the same distance away, 100 klicks on Highway One. Phu Bai to the north and Chu Lai to the south. Being new in country, no one could relate to how far a klick was compared to a mile, but they were about to find out. It was the terminology of the theater. Why some flew and others rode in a truck, was anyone's guess. That answer was above their paygrade.

"Sneed, Briggs, Leahy, Wood, Pfeiffer, Trakas. 12th Marines. Cannon cockers. You're over on the other side of Hill 327." Jackman pointed at the hill that Briggs thought should be called a mountain. He could see the radio antennas and a small building at the summit. A dirt road snaked its way up through the brown and green foliage.

"12th Marines has a transport unit down the road about half a klick. Grab your gear and make your way down there. They'll tell you what to do next."

Walking in the hundred-degree heat with a sea bag strapped over the shoulder was a challenge to itself. The sweat was pouring off them. 12th Marines was in a tent with a wooden floor and open sides. The temperature inside seemed twice as hot from the sun baking the canvas roof. They were quickly processed by another clerk / typist lance corporal who was sweating more than they were. No one bothered to get his name. No one cared. Clerk / typists seemed to be running the war.

"Hop on that deuce and a half." He pointed to the dull green transport truck parked 20 feet away. "Your drivers are around here somewhere. I'll round them up. They've been waiting for you guys to get here."

PFC Gaddis was the driver. PFC Weeks rode shotgun. They both had M-14s but had them well covered to protect from the dust that seemed to be everywhere.

The six newbies threw their sea bags into the back, climbed up and grabbed seats on the dusty benches on both sides of the bed.

As soon as the truck left the base it entered a stream of vehicles of all kinds that Briggs had never seen before, claptrap buses with passengers hanging off the sides or even riding on top, French made Peugeots, jitneys of different shapes and configurations, military trucks and jeeps, motor scooters and bicyclists who cut in and out of traffic seemingly unaware of how quickly they could be wiped out. The roads were narrow two lanes, part dirt with occasional stretches of asphalt that was badly in need of repair. The truck bounced through the potholes.

After a couple of turns they left the heavy traffic behind. They were on a dirt road heading west bordered on both sides by dry rice paddies. Vietnamese in black silk pajamas and cone hats were bent over at the waist working in the paddies oblivious to the nearby traffic.

"Shit. They told us at Pendleton that all the VC wore black pajamas. They didn't tell us everyone here wore black pajamas," Sneed commented. "How do you know who to shoot at?"

The truck entered a small village that consisted of run-down shacks and a few structures that appeared to be huts with straw roofs. A few old men and momma-sans were watching children play in the dirt.

There was no glass in the window frame between the driver's cab and the truck bed, so PFC Leahy leaned down and asked Weeks, who was riding shotgun, "What's the name of this place?" He had to shout to be heard.

Weeks turned around to answer. "It's got some bull shit Vietnamese name that none of us can pronounce. We call it Dogpatch. It's off limits. No skivvy houses. Just a bunch of rice farmers."

Occasional shacks thrown together with plywood, cardboard and sheet metal served as roadside businesses. Crudely made signs in pidgin English identified them as selling "suvneers," "col drnks," and "T-Shrts."

They passed one shack that did not need bad signage to indicate their line of work. Three young Vietnamese women were outside the hut yelling at the Marines that they were "number one boom boom" and "love you long time."

Weeks leaned out the truck window to yell back at them, "Nah, boom-boom number 10." He flashed a thumbs down as Gaddis laughed loudly. The girls held up their middle fingers in response.

They bounced along for another half hour passing two roadside check points manned by armed Marines in sandbagged bunkers. The truck was waved through.

They turned off the road and passed through the front gate of Fire-base Diamond, home to the First 8-Inch Howitzer Battery, 12th Marines, 3rd Marine Division. A hand painted yellow shield with red lettering read: "*1-8-H Semper Fidelis*" was attached to the small plywood guard shack on one side of a metal gate that swung open to allow the truck to pass. Two other handmade signs sitting one on top of the other featured an arrow pointing east "The World – 10,000 miles" and the other pointing north "Hanoi 500 miles."

Several strings of concertina wire ringed the base. Guard posts comprised of sheet metal roofs and sandbagged sides were positioned about every 50 yards around the perimeter.

The lethal looking, tank-like self-propelled howitzers were dug into separate positions aimed north, south and west. Danang was to the east so they did not shoot in that direction. They were now on the opposite side of Hill 327 from the airbase.

Two large bunkers fifty feet away from each other dominated the middle of the firebase. They served as the center of operations and fire control. Each was dug several feet into the ground and constructed of thick plank lumber protected on its sides and top by layers of sandbags.

Troop tents, with open sides and wood floors, each housing about 12 men, were purposely positioned in a haphazard pattern around the base. No structure was close enough to another to be damaged by one incoming explosive.

A few other buildings seemed more permanent with wooden sides, real doors and metal roofs. They housed clubs for enlisted and officers, as well as a small armory.

PFC Weeks leaned back to yell through the missing window – "Welcome Home Boys. Your all expenses paid trip to Firebase Diamond. Cocked and Locked."

CHAPTER 18

April 1966
Firebase Diamond
I Corps - Republic of Vietnam

Vietnam War Timeline: 1ˢᵗ Battalion, 3ʳᵈ Marines conduct Operation Orange, a Search and Destroy Mission in Quang Nam Province 40 miles southwest of Danang. Viet Cong losses were reported as 57 killed and 61 captured; friendly were 18 killed and 92 wounded.

"Corporal Briggs! The major wants to see you. On the double."

PFC Larry Risdon was a suck up little shit who was the battery commander's runner and do everything assistant.

Back in boot camp Risdon had been picked out by his drill instructors as having natural abilities for providing personal service. Positive evaluations in his personnel jacket resulted in that sort of assignment following him throughout his enlistment. He reminded Briggs of Truman Lipsky back in 3/8.

Briggs was cleaning his newly issued M-14 and four magazines. The parts were laid out on his bunk along with 80 rounds of 7.62 mm ammunition. He didn't immediately respond to Risdon, trying instead to figure out if this was some sort of an emergency, if he should take a couple minutes to put the rifle back together or whether he could leave it there to be finished later.

Risdon was standing at the tent door waiting for a response. "Did you hear me corporal? The major wants you now, not tomorrow."

"Yeah. I heard you PFC. Don't get a rag on. I have to put my rifle back together and then I'll be there."

Risdon stomped out obviously pissed at what he considered disrespect of him was disrespect of the Commanding Officer.

"Who the fuck was that?" Briggs asked the only other person in the tent at that time.

"He's the C.O.'s house mouse," answered Corporal Dana Smiley. "His nose is so far up Bo's ass that he thinks he is the C.O."

"Bo" was Major J. Beauregard Spencer, battery commanding officer.

"You might want to kick it into gear. Risdon will whisper some bad shit into Bo's ear and then you'll be digging yourself out of a hole right off the bat. I'll put your rifle back together for you."

"Shouldn't I have my weapon with me when I show up at the C.O.'s hooch?"

"Here take mine. He won't know the difference."

"Thanks Smiley. What do you figure he wants me for?"

"Beats me. Maybe you've been selected for a special mission to sneak into North Vietnam to assassinate Ho Chi Minh."

"Yeah. Right." Briggs grunted a short laugh.

"Shit, Bo didn't talk to me for three weeks after I got here. Then he called me Corporal Sweeney instead of Smiley. I was hoping I could do my whole tour before he found out I was here."

Briggs grabbed Smiley's rifle and web belt with full ammo pouches, popped on his soft cover and headed across the compound. The command hooch was about 200 yards away. Monsoon season had passed a month before Briggs arrived and the ground had lost all its moisture and turned into hard clay that made walking easier. A gray overcast provided a relatively comfortable temperature in the high 80s.

Briggs had only been in the unit three days and he was not sure how uptight Major Spencer would be about military protocol, so he figured he better play it by the book. Briggs banged on the wooden door.

"Sir, Corporal Briggs requests permission to enter, Sir!" Briggs hadn't spoken like that since he left boot camp, most of his other COs being lax about military decorum.

"Enter!" The one-word command was spoken as if he was back at the Marine Corps Recruit Depot - San Diego.

Major Spencer was sitting at a field desk with his head down looking at some papers as Briggs took his cover off and stepped smartly in front of him snapping to attention. Smiley's rifle was strapped over his right shoulder per protocol.

"Sir, Corporal Briggs reporting as ordered, Sir."

"At ease corporal. I'll be with you in a second." The CO briefly acknowledged Briggs with an amused look but returned quickly to the papers in front of him.

"Where the fuck do I put my John Hancock on this, First Sergeant?"

Briggs was aware of others in the hooch but kept his eyes straight ahead.

First Sergeant Michael Callahan appeared and pointed to the paper.

"Here...and here, Sir. Just your initials will do. Then sign it at the bottom," Callahan directed.

"Ah. Got it. Okay. Thanks." He handed the papers back to Callahan then looked up at Briggs. Major Spencer had a bullet shaped head that looked too big for his body. His hair was cut to the nub. No one in Vietnam had good hair. No reason for it.

"Corporal Briggs." He studied Briggs for a minute. Briggs was not sure if he was supposed to respond. Spencer looked down at his desk, shuffled a few more papers and came up with what Briggs could tell was his personnel record.

Spencer kept his eyes on Briggs' records: "You're a 2533 – radio / telegraph operator. CW. Morse code. Nobody uses that shit anymore. That's for boy scouts."

"Yes sir."

"Volunteered for Vietnam. Now why the fuck would you do something like that son?"

"Well sir, I was..."

"I know, you wanted to serve your country, kill commies, protect the folks at home. I do not want to hear about that shit.

"Briggs, I need a driver. Someone that knows how to operate a jeep on these water boo paths they call roads over here. Somebody that can get me around without getting me killed. Hell, the last driver I had scared the shit out of me.

"I want a radio operator for this job not some fucking cannon cocker. Are you up for this Briggs?"

"Yes sir." Briggs knew he did not have any choice in the matter.

"You come highly recommended. You better not fuck this up."

"Sir? Not sure what you mean by being highly recommended."

Spencer nodded towards the First Sergeant and another person sitting in the back of the tent. It was Gunnery Sergeant Ernie Lincoln.

"Gunny Lincoln? You told me this was one squared away Marine, right?"

"I did sir. If he fucks this up, I'll kick his ass back to the states."

Lincoln and Briggs smiled at each other. "Hello Gunny. When did you get here?" Lincoln stood. They shook hands.

"I figured since I talked you into coming over here, that I better follow my own advice. I couldn't bear the thought of you getting your ass shot off without me at least being somewhere in the vicinity. Just got in this morning. You can't get away from me son. The Marine Corps works in mysterious ways. Good to see you again."

"Okay, let's knock off this buddy fuck thing. Thanks, Gunny, for the recommendation. Briggs go see that little weenie Risdon and he will fill you in on my vehicle. It's your job to keep that radio working. I'll be heading out later this afternoon to division so stay close by. That's it for now."

Briggs snapped to attention, "Aye aye sir." He did an about face worthy of a parade ground Marine and stepped out into the bright daylight, having to stop for a moment to allow his eyes to adjust after the darkness of the command hooch.

When he got back to his tent Smiley had his M-14 back in one piece. He was laying on his own bunk smoking a cigarette. The sun had emerged from the clouds and had begun beating on the canvas roof. The temperature in the tent was reaching sauna level.

"Did you get your secret mission," Smiley asked.

"Yeah but if I told you what it was then I'd have to kill you," Briggs responded. "I'm the CO's new driver."

"Oh shit. Good luck on that one. He gets a new driver about every other week. Last week he left with Walt Ackerman driving. Ackerman's a PFC, gun crew guy. When they got back Ack was in the passenger seat and Bo was driving the Jeep himself. Ack said the old man had a shit fit when he made a U turn and almost got wiped out by a deuce and a half. Of course, Ack's not the sharpest tack of the bunch. Not sure I would want to ride with him either."

"Ack was glad to be fired. In fact, everyone who has been his driver was glad to get sacked. Bo's looking for medals you know. He doesn't give a shit if you're an unintended casualty if he gets his Silver Star or Navy Cross dead or alive. You want to keep your head down."

Briggs processed this without comment. He decided to change the subject.

"Why do they call this place Firebase Diamond? Is that Lou Diamond?"

Lou Diamond was known as Mr. Marine, a crusty gunnery sergeant who became a battlefield legend in both the World Wars.

"Nah. Don't we wish. Homer Diamond was our first KIA. He was a lance corporal. He wasn't killed by any bad guys. He was on one of the gun crews. A loader. They had just thrown a shell into the barrel, slammed the breech shut, and then for whatever reason, Diamond stuck his head down behind the gun just as the lanyard was pulled. The recoil just about took his head off. It exploded.

"No one knows why he did what he did. Might have seen something he wanted to pick up or didn't think the breech was closed. They picked up his head with a spoon."

"Firebase Diamond isn't an official name. We are the only ones that call it that. Bo needed to create a hero. He has this thing about heroes. He wants to be one too."

CHAPTER 19

May 1966
I Corps - Republic of Vietnam

Vietnam War Timeline: Continuing unrest resulted in U.S. Marines facing off against pro-Buddhist ARVN soldiers as the South Vietnam government regained control of Danang. In the fighting 150 ARVN soldiers were killed while 23 Americans were wounded. It was difficult for the Americans to understand who they were fighting since the ARVN were supposed to be their allies.

Briggs had been in country three weeks and felt like he had driven Bo everywhere in the Greater Danang Metropolitan Area. The major went someplace every day.

Several times a week there were meetings at I Corps Headquarters on the Danang side of Hill 327. Briggs dropped Bo off then found a parking spot with the other drivers. They had nothing to do during this time but to shoot the shit. They listened to the Armed Forces Network on pocket sized transistor radios. Most of the programming was country and western music with a 10-minute break for news each hour.

A couple times Briggs saw the already legendary I Corps commander, General Lewis Walt as he entered or left the building. Walt was a big man, a former college football player. Briggs felt like he had just seen Babe Ruth.

Other trips were to visit the gun crews that were deployed with infantry units as far as 25 miles outside of Danang. Those trips took them to remote areas north, south and west. Bo showed no reluctance to direct Briggs into off road and unchartered territory saying that he wanted to find suitable sites for new artillery emplacements. He did not seem concerned about their safety. Briggs always kept his M-14 next to him in case he needed it quickly.

Some mornings they had to wait for roads to be swept of mines before they could proceed. Heavy metal plates on the floor of the jeep were supposed to provide protection but Briggs had little faith that he and Bo would ever walk again after hitting a mine. He was sure that the entire jeep and its passengers would be obliterated. He tried to not dwell on that possibility.

Bo carried a large sack full of candies. As they passed through villages, dirty, half naked children would run next to the Jeep shouting for treats. Bo threw handfuls of the individually wrapped candies to the kids. Briggs watched through his rearview mirror as the kids scrambled for the candies. He always wondered if they would get run over by following traffic but so far that had not happened.

Once a week there was a trip to the main PX to replenish Bo's candy supply and other personal items. Briggs noticed that each visit Bo also purchased a couple fifths of Jack Daniels that he would carefully wrap in a tee-shirt and stuff into one of the Jeep's compartments. When they got back to Firebase Diamond, Bo personally transported that cargo into his hooch while Briggs, or Risdon, were responsible for his other items.

The back of the Jeep consisted of a bench seat and a AN/MRC-38 Radio that was always tuned to the main battery frequency so Bo could monitor all radio traffic. Bo's call sign was Ringo Six. The CO was always "the Six." The XO was Five. Everyone else of importance had their own Ringo call sign including the deployed units.

There was not a lot of talk between Briggs and the Six even though they were stuck in the same vehicle together several hours a day. A major did not have friendly conversations with a corporal, especially this major. And a corporal certainly did not start jawboning with a major. Bo spent a lot of time talking on the radio and listening to the other unit communications.

With one primary exception, Bo seemed pleased with Briggs' driving. Once Briggs tried to pass an ARVN troop truck in a busy section of Highway One near the Danang Airbase. Bo stopped him.

"What the fuck are you doing corporal? Stay in your own lane. Things will open up." There was disgust in Bo's voice. Briggs noticed that he spoke to most people the same way.

Bo had been right. Just as Briggs pulled back into the right lane, a five-ton U.S. Army truck went by in the other direction. They would have ended up as a hood ornament.

"Briggs, that's the first dumb ass thing you've done since you've been my driver. Don't let it happen again or you'll be filling sandbags and burning shitters. You got that?"

"Yes sir," Briggs replied.

Briggs had lasted longer than any driver. He kept the Jeep immaculate, made sure the radio was working, seemed to find the best parking areas and quickly learned how to get where they needed to go. Briggs studied the maps each day before their ventures to make sure he knew exactly where they were headed. Getting lost would have been the ultimate sin.

Despite the danger of getting blown up by a mine or being shot at, which seemed to be more of a minor annoyance, Briggs liked the job. It kept him out of the daily bullshit that was part of garrison life reinforcing bunkers, filling sandbags, standing guard duty, maintaining radios and vehicles.

The worse job always assigned to the lowest PFC and supervised by a junior NCO was having to burn out the shitters two or three times a week. It was somebody's idea of a joke that this task was always scheduled on Sunday mornings after religious services were held by the roving chaplain.

Telling Briggs this would be his fate if he failed as a driver was the ultimate threat that the Six could make. The process required pouring motor oil into the pits and setting them on fire. The pit crew was required to stand nearby while the flames burned down to make sure the outhouses didn't catch on fire in the process. No one stood downwind from the toxic smoke.

The other job that everyone tried to avoid was spraying the brush cover around the perimeter. This job was completed with a back-mounted tank and spray hose. There was no possible way to avoid inhaling the mist and getting it on skin and clothes. They all noticed how it caused rashes and breathing problems for a few days afterwards.

Briggs enjoyed being close to command. He felt he was in the know since the Six carried on a lot of business in the Jeep. Briggs, of course, was expected to keep his mouth shut.

Often, they had a passenger or two crammed into the back seat. It was usually another officer or senior NCO who needed to be somewhere and would hitch a ride with the Six. Briggs noticed that Bo didn't have lengthy conversations with them either.

Driving in the hot open vehicle on dirt roads left him at the end of each day covered in dust and in need of something besides warm canteen water to clear his dry throat.

The shower was in a small metal building with two 50-gallon barrels and a water heater mounted on the roof linked to shower heads below. The Seabees had rigged these showers up all over Vietnam. Keeping the tank full of water and the heater working was another shit job assigned daily to a different PFC or lance corporal.

No one went to the shower without his weapon, so a rifle rack was stationed just outside for easy access in case of an attack. There is nothing deadlier than a buck naked, pissed-off Marine with his rifle, shower shoes and towel.

Off hours drinking was done in one of two tents. The officers and NCOs drank in one tent. Everyone else in another. Over time each club was improved with furniture and accessories scrounged from other units. A daily ice delivery kept the beer chilled. Gasoline generators provided electricity to the clubs and some of the troop tents until 2200 hours each night. Then the base went dark.

Supposedly each unit in Vietnam was allocated two beers per man per day. 1ˢᵗ 8" Howitzer Battery drew a daily quota for one-hundred and eighty men. The fact that over fifty of them were deployed with other units was never a factor. The extra beers were a bonus. Plus, cases of beer could be purchased at the PX. There never seemed to be a limitation on how much beer was available.

Fire missions in support of infantry operations up to 20 miles away were conducted throughout the day and night. The boom of the howitzers and the ground shaking became routine to those not in the gun pits.

"I could sleep through a hurricane," Smiley commented one day. "Never heard the H & I last night."

"Harassment and Interdiction" were single random rounds fired at pre-selected targets at various times during the night meant to keep the enemy on edge. They never knew when a 200-pound shell was going to drop in their lap. The results were rarely noted or reported by forward observers.

Briggs was not exempt from radio watches. He was committed to the Six each day, so he was usually given a four-hour watch either beginning at twenty hundred hours ending at midnight, or from midnight to zero four hundred hours.

Radio watches were conducted in the Fire Direction Center bunker which was in the geographical center of the base. The Seabees had created a hole ten feet underground, reinforced it with four by eight planks on the sides, floor and roof. The Marines fortified it with sandbags, a job that never ended. No one seemed to know exactly how many layers of sandbags it would take to keep from being destroyed by enemy mortar and artillery fire.

Briggs worried more about VC getting through the wire and throwing a grenade into the FDC. There was no place to hide. It was just a big open room with one way in and one way out.

Gunny Lincoln took over as the NCO in charge of the communications section much to the displeasure of Sergeant Al Latham but was welcomed by the rest of the platoon.

Latham was a lanky E-5 with seven years in the Marine Corps who seemed to be in a perpetually foul mood. His most prominent feature were nasty looking teeth that caused him a lot of discomfort and many trips to the division dental unit.

He had done little to organize the platoon. Watch schedules were rarely posted. More than once Briggs was rousted out of his sack because no one had told him he had the duty at zero four hundred. Equipment maintenance had gotten lax. Latham yelled a lot, but few listened. The other NCOs who were junior to Latham were quickly cut off when they tried to help manage the platoon.

One would have thought Latham would be pleased that he was no longer in charge, but it was obvious he was pissed and resented Gunny Lincoln who brought an experienced and organized management style to the platoon.

CHAPTER 20

June 1966
I Corps - Republic of Vietnam

Vietnam War Timeline: Operation Liberty kicked off with heavy artillery shelling in front of the advancing 9th Marines. VC resistance was described as "scattered and ineffective." The regiment claimed to have recovered 40 square miles in the Danang enclave.

Firebase Diamond was Major J. Beauregard "Bo" Spencer's world. This war was his last hurrah. He needed to leave Vietnam as a battalion commander. That would require a promotion to lieutenant colonel and some battlefield decorations.

Bo had enlisted in the Marine Corps during World War Two and became an officer during the Korean Conflict. Officers who began their careers as enlisted Marines and were later commissioned were known as mustangs.

Mustangs were viewed differently than officers who were trained at the academies or ROTC. They were relics of the Old Corps. The best a mustang could hope for was to make full bird colonel and that was a stretch.

Like other mustangs, Bo had a tattoo that he got during his enlisted days, something that was frowned upon by the modern officer corps. Mustangs covered them up as much as possible even wearing long sleeved shirts in the heart of summer. Bo's only tattoo was a Marine

Corps emblem high on his right bicep that he got in Tijuana when he was a young corporal. At least it wasn't something more graphic like a naked woman or a snake wrapped around a dagger.

Being a major with 23 years of service, Bo knew his time was running out. He had been passed over for lieutenant colonel twice. One more time and he would be forced to retire. He watched bitterly as majors with less seniority pass him by in the promotion line and the opportunity for better assignments.

He and his wife Maddie exchanged letters about once a month just to let each other know they were each still alive. She lived in a small ranch house they had bought ten years ago in Oceanside, California, near Camp Pendleton. She stayed there regardless of where he was stationed. She had her own life to live.

Their two kids were grown and gone. His daughter Vickie had disappeared into the hippie community of San Francisco. They heard from her occasionally when she was arrested for drug possession or vagrancy. She had adopted a new street name calling herself Soledad, as a tribute to friends of hers who were incarcerated in Soledad Prison in northern California.

Their son Jason and Bo had not spoken to each other in several years. When Jason had gotten his draft notice, he fled to Canada where he was active in the anti-war movement advising other young men on how to avoid the draft. He also smoked a lot of dope.

Bo needed to make something happen in the twilight of his career. Running an effective artillery battery was not enough. He particularly thought about it at night when he would sip Jack Daniels in the privacy of his commander's hooch.

In the eight months he had been in Vietnam the battery had seen zero face to face action with the enemy. The infantry got all that action. Like everyone in country he couldn't tell a good guy from a bad guy. There had been suspicious activity around the perimeter at nights. A nervous 19-year-old PFC saw things that move in the night and would light up the sky with a parachute flare. Those not on duty would immediately run to their fighting positions. But so far, there had been no attacks on their position.

An Army firebase of 105 mm howitzers just two miles away got hit one night. VC in the wire killed six American soldiers and blew up two shacks. One howitzer was lost to an explosive being shoved into the breech.

The CO received some shrapnel wounds but continued to lead his troops in repulsing the attack. The next morning, they counted 11 dead VC. The CO was awarded a purple heart and was nominated for a Bronze Star. Bo yearned for a similar experience.

"Risdon! Find Briggs. I'll be ready in 15." Risdon checked in with Bo every morning by 0700 and every half hour after that until the major decided what his agenda was for the day. It was now 0730.

Bo thought Risdon was the ultimate kiss ass who made a perfect house mouse. He never felt a need to say anything nice to Risdon. Because of his sharp facial features, Bo thought the slight PFC looked like a rat.

Briggs pulled the radio jeep up exactly at 0743 hours. It was his practice to always be two minutes early. It was a clear day meaning that the sun would soon be heating up the tents making life inside like being in a sauna.

Two six-man patrols were sent out each morning to look for any overnight VC activity around the perimeter. They were expected to be out at least two hours checking the fence line and patrolling a couple miles out through the local villages.

Nothing ever happened on these patrols which caused the men at times to become dangerously lackadaisical, something they were constantly warned against. The NCO in charge, a sergeant or at least a corporal, would nag them to be alert. This was not just a walk in the countryside.

Back at the firebase, gun crews were manning their positions in case of a fire mission. They constantly cleaned and oiled the artillery and ammunition, as well as caring for their personal weapons and equipment.

There was a daily run with the tanker truck into Danang for clean water. Everyone was allocated four full canteens each day and strict water discipline was enforced. That water was also to be used for shaving. Shaving with cold water without ripping your face open was part of life in Vietnam.

There was never a shortage of volunteers for the water run as it meant a day away from routine work parties. It could mean a stop by the main PX and it was not unknown for them to take a quick detour to a convenient skivvy house. One man stayed on guard in the truck while the other enjoyed a boom boom. "Where's the old man going today," Briggs asked Risdon.

"You're not authorized to know," Risdon answered. That was Risdon's way of trying to sound more important than Briggs.

"What the fuck? How could I not be authorized to know? I'm driving him," Briggs responded showing his irritation with the house mouse. "Never mind. I don't know why I bothered to ask."

Bo emerged from his hooch. He was armed with the standard military 45 caliber pistol in a holster on his web belt which was attached to suspenders. He carried a map case and binoculars.

"Let's go corporal. We're headed to division." This was the weekly meeting Bo was required to attend.

"Bullshit progress reports," was all that Bo would share with Briggs about the content of the meeting.

Division headquarters was at the bottom of Hill 327 about six miles away on unnamed dirt roads which had already been swept for mines by one of the engineer units. Occasionally, they missed one. Briggs prayed that his jeep would not be the one to discover it.

Bo kept discussion to a minimum. He and Briggs were comfortable in their mutual silence. They monitored the radio traffic on the MRC-38. Most of it was routine administrative stuff until one fire mission was called in by a forward observer who had seen VC activity in Quang Ni province southwest of Danang.

It took the FO two rounds to walk the shells in on target before he radioed "fire at will." When five more rounds were fired, he said "cease fire. Mission accomplished."

Briggs always admired the calm, cool delivery of the FO's who he did not know but could see them in his mind's eye, huddled under a tree or behind a rock on a high spot overlooking an enemy position.

After another five minutes, the FO called in the results of the mission. "Three KIA. Two vehicles destroyed."

Briggs knew that report would create a lot of whooping among the folks back at the FDC and in the gun pit. This was their job to kill people.

It would also put a spring in Bo's step. He was headed to a meeting at division and could report a body count. That would mean Bo Spencer would get an "attaboy."

CHAPTER 21

June 1966
I Corps - Republic of Vietnam

Vietnam Timeline: American KIA during the month of June 1966 were 683. Over 2,700 Americans were killed during the first six months of the year.

Mail call was the most exciting part of the day. Anyone who wasn't on duty showed up for mail call. Corporal Sneed was the mail clerk. He made a daily run to Division Headquarters to pick up the mail. For ten minutes each day he was the most popular man in the unit.

He stood on the top step of the admin hooch and call out names flipping letters through the air.

"Beavers."

"Yo. Here." A letter sailed through the air.

"Crooks."

"Here."

"Johnson."

"I'll take it. He's on duty."

On it would go until the stack disappeared.

"That's all for today ladies. See you tomorrow."

Since he had left Lejeune, Briggs and Brenda had exchanged a couple of letters that had been distinctly free of any signs of affection or discussion of the future. Briggs felt he might as well be corresponding with the pen pal he had been assigned in the fourth grade.

Brenda had graduated in May. She mentioned moving to New York to find a job but was short on details. Briggs sent her a note of congratulations. She had responded saying she thought of him often and hoped he was safe. There was no talk of missing each other. The relationship was on hold.

Briggs felt they were living in different worlds and even though he carried a picture of Brenda in his wallet, his memories of her were getting foggy.

This day all that Sneed had for him was a letter from his mother with news clippings from the Battle Creek Enquirer reporting on the recent spring flood of the Kalamazoo River that flowed through downtown. She felt the newspaper could explain things better than she could. Other than that, everyone was fine.

Briggs had the day off from Bo. The CO spent the day with the X-O, Captain Mains, and Gunny Lincoln reviewing the perimeter defenses, fields of fire, the guard posts and the condition of the concertina wire. They always checked to make sure no wise ass VC had turned the claymore mines around, which would send the blast in the direction of friendly fire.

They decided two new guard posts needed to be erected to fill in where there was too much distance between existing positions. That was a job for a PFC supervised by a corporal.

No one knew exactly how long Firebase Diamond would remain where it was but while First 8-Inch Howitzers owned this piece of property, they were expected to improve the defenses and living conditions daily. The next unit to live there, if any, would benefit from their hard work.

When he wasn't driving the Six, Briggs was expected to be in the comm shack which was usually a good place to hide when work party assignments were being handed out. Communicators were viewed as having special skills, so they rarely got scooped up.

The downside of being there was having to work with Sergeant Latham, who was in a piss poor mood as usual. He assigned Briggs to work with newly arrived PFCs Whitman and Atwood. The Marine

Corps had reduced boot camp to eight weeks to get more men to Vietnam quicker. There was no occupational specialty training being provided which meant that the cherries were expected to learn on the job. More hand holding time by Latham, Briggs and the other veterans.

The Marine Corps had begun to take draftees, one out of four, the others were headed to the Army. Whitman was the first draftee in the unit. He had gone to college for two years, University of Wisconsin, which he let everyone know about, as if it meant he was smarter than them. The fact that he must have flunked out, why else would he have ended up in Vietnam, didn't seem to affect his attitude. Whitman was not a happy camper which meant he had to be watched closely.

A patrol went out each afternoon. The time was varied in case they were being watched. Briggs volunteered to carry the radio. The patrol leader was Sergeant Eric Golubski. He was a professional Marine with nine years in the Corps including a stint as a drill instructor at Parris Island. Anyone who served on the drill field retains a high level of respect with the troops throughout his career.

Golubski was one of the original members of the unit from when it left Okinawa in the fall of 1965 to come to Vietnam. He was now on the list to be promoted to staff sergeant and there were some rumors that he might even get a field commission to second lieutenant.

Eight Marines armed with M-14s, and one M-79 grenade launcher left through the main gate at 1545 hours. Briggs carried the PRC-25 radio on his back, the handset dangling by a strap from his helmet. The PRC-25 had replaced the PRC-10 as the basic Marine Corps field radio. It was smaller, lighter, more durable and communicated more effectively over longer distance.

He traded his M-14 for the standard .45 caliber pistol as it was difficult to carry a rifle and a radio at the same time though he would miss the firepower if they ever got into a scramble.

They walked a minimum of twenty feet apart. PFC Manata had the point with Lance Corporal Nunnally covering the rear. For about a mile they stuck to the well-traveled dirt road that connected Firebase Diamond to all points north and south. They were more in danger of being hit by a military truck than they were an attack by the VC.

Eventually Manata led the patrol onto a trail towards a collection of huts about a half mile away that was surrounded by dikes and rice paddies, still dry at this time of year.

"Ringo Eight this is Ringo One. Radio check." Briggs was supposed to check in every 15 minutes or else base would call him. He had sat on the other end of this transmission many times.

"This is Ringo Eight. Loud and Clear," Briggs responded. He added a quick location report.

"Roger. Out," was the answer from base.

As they passed through the village the Vietnamese paid little attention. A few squatted like baseball catchers around their cook stoves. Three small children played a game in the dirt. Two old women feigned modesty pulling tunics around them tightly and watched with quiet eyes as the patrol passed. Each man on the patrol looked intently into the huts as much out of curiosity as expecting to find any danger.

A water buffalo, known as a water boo, stood in a small corral keeping an eye on the Americans, who in turn kept an eye on him. These beasts of burden were invaluable to the Vietnamese farmers. They were known to be skittish and reports of having attacked American soldiers were common.

The rumor was that the animals could sense that the Americans, unlike the Vietnamese, were meat eaters. A previous patrol had run into a particularly aggressive water boo and had to shoot it. The U.S. government then was required to pay the farmer a thousand dollars. To Vietnamese peasants that was a huge amount of money, more than enough to buy a new water buffalo and some extra luxuries.

A young man, about 20 years old, appeared riding a bicycle quickly through the ville. He seemed as surprised to see the Marines as they were him. Briggs could see everyone's increased awareness.

Golubski stopped him and asked to see identification. The man spoke enough English that he understood what Golubski wanted. He argued with him for a few moments before pulling out his wallet and flashing something that seemed to satisfy the sergeant. The look on the man's face showed his displeasure of being forced by a foreign soldier to show his ID in his own country.

The suspicion they all had, the man being of military age, if he wasn't ARVN then he must be VC.

Briggs felt this whole exercise of walking through the village was absurd and an invasion of people's privacy. He had no idea what they were looking for and he suspected neither did Golubski.

They left the ville and crossed a couple of smaller dry rice paddies, staying off the dikes. About a half mile out they entered a small thicket of bushes and trees. Manata held up his hand and dropped down low. The rest of the patrol did the same.

Golubski moved up to talk with Manata. They pointed to a hedgerow that bordered the other side of a large rice paddy about 300 yards away. Manata had seen movement. Golubski told the patrol to form a perimeter while he decided what to do next.

"Briggs. Let base know our coordinates and that we're holding to check out some bees in a bush," Golubski ordered. He pulled out his map and gave Briggs their location.

"Ringo One. This is Ringo eight. Holding at 6344 8217. Wait five."

"This is Ringo One. Roger. Repeat coordinates 6344 8217."

"Roger."

The patrol remained huddled while Manata and Golubski kept their eyes focused on the hedgerow. Two men dressed in black pajamas emerged and began picking their way along the paddy dike heading in the direction of the patrol. One of them was carrying something long and black that looked like a rifle. He seemed to use it occasionally as a walking stick helping him maintain his balance on the narrow dyke. They had not seen the patrol.

"Pass the word," Golubski whispered. "Gooks at 12 o'clock. Everyone holds." The entire patrol turned at the ready to watch the men approach.

When they were about 20 yards away Golubski stood up and held his hand up as if saying "stop." They did. The looks on their faces were of total surprise.

There was a long moment of silence as everyone tried to decide what to do next. The man with the stick started to raise it as if he were holding up his hands. That's when shots were fired behind Briggs. Everyone then let loose. The two men were cut down immediately.

"Cease fire! Cease fire!" Golubski hollered. He had to yell two more times before the firing stopped.

"What the fuck? Shit!" Golubski ran out to check the two bodies. They were riddled. Golubski reached down and picked up a long black stick the one man had been using for balance.

"I never gave an order to shoot. Who the fuck fired first?"

No one responded. Then Nunally pointed at PFC Harold Grizzle, a lanky eyesore who stood wide eyed with a speck of drool leaking from the corner of his mouth.

"I thought they were going to shoot."

"With what? His fucking stick?" Golubski hollered. "What the fuck were you thinking man?"

"They wore black pajamas."

"Everyone wears black pajamas. Or haven't you fucking noticed?"

Golubski circled the bodies muttering "fuck" to himself. These were the first two dead bodies Briggs had ever seen other than in a funeral home. They didn't look like real people laying so still and already drained of color.

"Grizzle. You're a fucking dumb shit. How the hell are we going to explain this," Golubski said.

"Briggs. Call this in. Two enemy KIA. Find out what the fuck we do now."

Briggs had a five-minute conversation with more than one person at Firebase Diamond. "We're supposed to hang loose and wait here. Bo is coming out to inspect the damage."

Golubski ordered a perimeter defense formation while they waited. It took twenty minutes for Bo to show up with Captain Mains and

Gunny Lincoln. They had brought another jeep and four men with them.

They parked their vehicles about a quarter mile away and trudged over the dykes and through the dry paddies.

"What have we got here Sergeant?"

"Two gooks, Sir. We were in a defensive position over here in the trees. They came across the paddy. They didn't see us," Golubski was sure his ass was grass. He decided to say as little as possible not sure if he would be testifying in a court martial or not.

"Where are their weapons," Bo asked.

Golubski hesitated. "No weapons sir." He nodded at the black piece of wood lying on the ground next to the bodies.

"You thought they were going to beat you to death with that stick?"

Captain Mains laughed. A look from Bo cut him off. Gunny Lincoln stayed silent looking grim.

"You caught them getting ready to set some booby traps. You got to them before they got to that ville over there. They were going to kidnap the village chief. Kill the women and children. Don't you think that's what happened here sergeant?"

Golubski got the drift and was only too happy to agree with Bo's version of events. "Yes Sir. That's the way it happened."

Gunny Lincoln looked at Briggs and rolled his eyes. It was his way of asking Briggs if he could live with this story that they all knew was bull-shit.

Briggs rolled his eyes back and shrugged his shoulders. They knew each other well enough that this was the only communication they needed. It was hard for Briggs to think of these two teenagers as danger-ous enemy combatants. There was no evidence to point to their intent to cause harm to the Americans other than a large stick and black paja-mas.

Bo, Gunny Lincoln and Captain Mains talked it over among them-selves for a couple minutes.

"Briggs. Call base. Tell them to contact division to send out some body snatchers to take care of these two. Sergeant Golubski, your patrol will have to hang loose until they show up. Then get the fuck out of here and back to base. Good work men."

Bo led his entourage back to the vehicles. His after-action report would describe how the patrol had conducted a successful ambush. The number crunchers at division would ring up two more enemy KIA.

CHAPTER 22

July 4, 1966
I Corps - Republic of Vietnam

Vietnam War Timeline: Operation Hastings was launched in Quang Tri Province to push the NVA forces back across the DMZ. American military leaders called it an "unqualified success." U.S. casualties were 126 KIA.

The movie that night was Episode Seven, Season Four of "Combat," entitled "Hear No Evil," starring Vic Morrow as Sergeant Saunders and Rick Jason as Lieutenant Hanley. It was a movie under the stars. Anyone not on duty showed up with their helmet, weapon and a folding lawn chair purchased either at the PX or from one of the many roadside kiosks operated by entrepreneurial Vietnamese.

A end-of-his-career major sitting at a desk back at the Pentagon in Washington, 10,000 miles away, was in charge of troop entertainment and must have decided that the best way to keep warriors focused on the war was to provide them with movies in which the Americans always win.

Alternative entertainment consisted of episodes from "Gunsmoke," "The Rifleman," or "Bonanza." "Combat" always drew the largest audience. Everyone had their favorite character: Saunders, Hanley, Kirby, the French Canadian Caje, Littlejohn or Doc. "Caje, take the point" was a favorite phrase of Sergeant Saunders.

Kirby was the rebellious PFC who wielded a BAR (Browning Automatic Rifle), no longer standard issue in the Marine Corps, but missed by those who had fired it. Everyone got wounded, multiple times, but none of the main cast ever died. They always returned to duty with no lingering effects and a purple heart. That's how the warriors of Vietnam pictured themselves surviving their own wounds.

Movie season was during the dry summer months. Corporal Sneed picked up a movie twice a week at division headquarters. There was no rhyme or reason to the order in which they were dispersed. It didn't matter. Each episode was a mini drama that stood on its own. Even the officers joined the enlisted men in the nightly entertainment sometimes watching the same episode three nights in a row.

Sneed was the ultimate administrative NCO that every unit cherished. Among his many talents was keeping the movie projector running despite heat, humidity, dust and rain. He was also the only one that knew how to thread the film without breaking it or causing the projector to jam and burning the film in the middle of a key battle scene.

Days of the week didn't matter. July 4, 1966, was a Monday which meant it was a long weekend for people back in the states to enjoy parades, parties and a day off from work.

At Firebase Diamond it was just another war day. There were three fire missions before noon. After activity reports from one of the FO's reported that six enemy KIA had been caught in the open. Dropping a bomb on nameless, faceless Vietnamese fifteen miles away made it a good day's work.

Being a national holiday in the states, the cooks did their best to prepare a special meal. Steaks were grilled outside the mess tent on open fires. They weren't Prime A quality, but no one complained. It was better than warmed-over canned B Rations that was the usual nightly fare.

There was some thought that the VC and NVA might have a Fourth of July surprise planned. The guard posts had extra men in place that night.

Sneed started the movie just before sunset. It was plenty dark to be seen on the outside screen. Fourteen minutes into the movie was when the first mortar round landed.

It occurred at the same moment that Sergeant Saunders was knocked unconscious by an enemy grenade that exploded near him during a fire-fight.

At first, no one moved being unable to distinguish between fact and fiction, the movie and the real thing. When the second round landed three seconds later, there was no mistaking it for Hollywood sound effects.

"Incoming! Incoming!" Everyone had assigned positions in case of an attack. It would take them a while to find their way through the chaos without getting killed in the process.

The second round had scored a direct hit on the troop shower. Plywood and plumbing parts flew everywhere. The two water tanks dropped fifteen feet to the ground and burst open soaking the ground with one hundred gallons of steaming hot water. One Marine had been using the shower when it was hit. He was obliterated. His partial body parts were collected later to be sent home to his family for burial.

When the explosions occurred, Briggs had been sipping beer from a cup and enjoying the movie. The beer now soaked his shirt and pants.

As a senior radio operator and NCO, his first responsibility was to make his way to the FDC which was only about twenty-five yards from where he had hit the ground. Twenty seconds passed with no more incoming rounds, so he decided to make a run for it.

The guard posts had all started firing machine guns and M-14s. Flares were shot into the sky casting a ghostly light over the firebase. People were running in different directions trying to find cover in the sand bagged fighting positions.

Briggs entered a crowded and busy FDC. Bo was smoking a cigar and issuing orders to Captain Mains and First Sergeant Callahan who nodded automatically and said "yes sir" several times over.

Gunny Lincoln was talking on the land line to the guard posts and relaying information to Bo.

Second Lieutenant Al Burns was the fire command officer on duty. He and Sergeant Latham were hanging over the two radio operators, who despite the attack on Firebase Diamond needed to maintain communication nets with infantry units they were supporting. It seemed as if all of I Corps was experiencing Fourth of July fireworks. Firebase Diamond had to fight its own battle while continuing to complete fire missions.

"Sarge. Do you need me, or should I head out to one of the guard posts?"

Latham nodded briefly. "Go. We got it covered."

Before he could get out the door, Gunny Lincoln said: "Briggs, guard post six is doing a shitload of firing. Get out there and see what the fuck is happening. I have a feeling we have a couple of dipshits manning that post. They're not picking up the phone. Report back when you find out."

"Aye. Aye Gunny."

"Take ammo with you. They'll need it."

On his way out of the bunker Briggs grabbed a PRC-6 radio, walkie-talkie. It was calibrated to the battery radio net. He took it only if he needed a backup to the guard post wire communications.

Two more mortar rounds landed. One dropped near the officer's club blowing out one side of the plywood building. The canvas roof was left dangling.

The other round missed everything but threw plenty of shrapnel whizzing through the air designed to maim anyone who hadn't ducked.

The Marines manning the fifty caliber machine guns at every other guard post were either wiping out an entire NVA regiment or were just having fun pulling the trigger of one of the most lethal weapons in the world.

The artillery gun crews continued their fire missions supporting the infantry units. The howitzer blasts and the automatic weapons fire were deafening. Briggs heard at least two claymore mine blasts as well.

Briggs stopped first at one of the secondary ammo dumps that were positioned around the compound. He grabbed an ammo box containing one thousand M-14 rounds. It weighed about thirty pounds.

The closest guard post was number five. Briggs had to traverse a lot of open space trudging through soft sand. There was no place to hide. Carrying his own rifle, the PRC-6, and the ammo box he felt like he was hardly moving and was a fat, easy target for some enemy soldier who he was sure had him lined up in his sights. He thought his life would be over before the next step.

When he was about twenty feet from the post he was challenged.

"Halt. Who goes there?"

Briggs felt like he was in a movie scene. People don't really talk like that in the middle of a battle, do they? With all the noise he was surprised they could hear each other.

To be safe, he stopped and yelled as loud as he could: "Corporal Briggs. I've got ammo for you."

"What? I can't hear you. Say again."

Oh fuck, Briggs thought. What if I was really a VC or NVA, would this dipshit be having a conversation with me? He decided to keep yelling while moving forward and take the chance that he wouldn't get shot.

He ducked his head as he entered the guard post and pushed aside PFC Phillip Cole, who had joined the unit just two days before. Cole was scared shitless.

"What are you guys shooting at out there?" Briggs asked.

"I don't know. Everyone else is shooting," Cole said.

"That's no fucking answer."

Cole's partner Lance Corporal Steve Worsham continued firing sporadically. His M-14 was on semi-automatic so at least he wasn't burning up a shitload of ammo. The M-14 on automatic was virtually uncontrollable so only a few were issued with a selector switch. If it didn't jam it could pour out the twenty-round magazine in less than five seconds. Hitting something was another question.

Multiple parachute flares had been launched since the first mortar round landed. They bathed the landscape in an eerie greenish - yellowish light. Each flare lasted about a minute, followed immediately by another.

"Let me see what the fuck you guys are shooting at out there." He pushed Cole aside and kneeled behind the sandbags next to Worsham who stopped firing. Briggs looked out through the gun ports. He could not see any incoming fire.

Because the parachute flares wiggled on their way down, everything on the landscape tended to look like it was moving. All Briggs could see was the concertina wire and trees in the far distance. The field of fire was open for at least two hundred yards.

"Post six keeps firing at something," Worsham whispered as if he was going to give away his position by talking too loudly. The .50 caliber thirty yards away continued to pour out the rounds. Briggs felt he could have walked on the bright line made by the tracers that were every fifth round of the ammo belt.

"Cole. Grab some of the ammo from the box. The two of you cool the firing unless you actually see something. Keep your eyes peeled out there.

"I need to pay a visit to your next-door neighbors and find out what the fuck is going on over there."

Briggs grabbed the ammo box and started a low run towards post six. Forgetting that fighting holes had been dug approximately halfway between each guard post, he found one unmanned when he tumbled into it head over asshole.

He heard himself involuntarily emit a loud "ummpf" as his 180 pounds slammed into the hole.

His ankle turned as it hit the bottom sending a shooting pain up his leg. His head hit the side of the hole. His face dug into the ground filling his mouth and eyes full of dirt. He was sure he had momentarily lost consciousness.

At first, he thought he had been shot. It took him a minute to confirm that he wasn't wounded.

When he fell, he dropped the ammo box shattering the clasp that held it closed. M-14 rounds now were lying on the ground. His rifle was still slung over his shoulder, but the flash suppressor had dug into the dirt and it would need to be cleaned before he fired it.

When he fell, he landed on the hard metal casing of the PRC-6 which was between his ribs and the ground. He thought he may have cracked a rib. His helmet had protected his head, but he still could feel a lump forming. He touched it lightly. His hand came away with blood. He pulled out a handkerchief and quickly blotted the cut.

He laid there without moving for another five minutes until he could get his wits about him. "Fuck," he said out loud to himself. It made him feel better.

He scooped up as many rounds as he could throwing them back in the can, tested his sore ankle which he could feel swelling up in his boot, and limped toward post six, now only about twenty yards away.

No one challenged him this time. Briggs arrived unannounced launching himself through the back opening, tripping over a pack and taking another tumble. The reinforced fighting hole was dug down four feet and covered with lumber, scrap metal and sandbags.

He scared the shit out of the two Marines on post who had been totally focused with what was in front of them.

"What the fuck?" yelled PFC Art Dolan who immediately turned his rifle on Briggs now laying on the ground.

Briggs looked up the barrel pointed at his head. "Don't shoot me you asshole. It's me. Briggs." He noticed that the .50 caliber had gone silent as he painfully picked himself up once more.

"What are you guys shooting at?"

"Anything that moves corporal. Anything that moves," Dolan replied. His partner PFC Jerry Neville, known by the nickname of "Neville Dog," a pun on the Marine nickname of Devil Dog, was behind the fifty caliber. He said nothing but kept his hands next to the butterfly trigger.

Briggs looked through the gun port. He saw the same nothingness that he saw at post five. Now that Neville wasn't shooting, he realized that all firing seemed to have ceased. Even the howitzers were quiet.

"Did you get any incoming?" Briggs asked.

"Yeah. Yeah. I think so," said Dolan. "We definitely saw something out there. Right Nev?" Neville nodded and grunted in agreement.

"What's going on at the other posts," Dolan asked.

"Not sure. I haven't heard anymore incoming. You were the only ones still firing. Why didn't you answer the field phone?"

"Didn't hear no ringing," Dolan said. Briggs figured with all the noise these guys were making it would have been impossible to hear a field phone jingling.

No one spoke for about a minute. They continued watching their sector.

"What happened to you corporal? You're bleeding. You get shot," Dolan asked.

"Not exactly. I just felt like I was. I'll be fine."

Briggs picked up the phone and rang the CP. Gunny Lincoln answered.

"This is Briggs. We've calmed down post six. Can't see anything out there now. These guys claim they saw some movement along the wire. I think they just decided to have some fun with the fifty. What's going on at the other posts?"

"Nada. All's quiet on the Western Front. We probably had a few VC on their way home for the night and decided to fuck with us. They high-tailed out after tossing those coconuts at us.

"Full alert all night. Stay where you are and keep those cowboys in check. I'll let you know if I need you."

The howitzer fire missions picked up again after midnight, but nothing more than normal. There was a lot of staring into the darkness. Flares lit up the sky every few minutes. The usual pre-planned H & I missions were fired each hour. No one slept.

At sunrise two patrols were sent out to walk the perimeter. The claymores had been set off by a dog. What was left of its corpse was draped over the concertina wire. It was the only evidence found of any battle the night before.

The suspected firing location of the mortar was discovered southwest of Firebase Diamond about a thousand yards out in a gully. The burnt grass showed signs of flashback and footprints disappeared into a nearby rice paddy.

The Seabees showed up and rebuilt the shower and a new officer's club in time for happy hour that night.

Briggs limped over to the medical tent to get patched up. He had to wait a half hour as the corpsmen were busy with the paperwork involved with the one Marine who was killed in the shower. Briggs needed basic first aid and a brace for his ankle. He was given a chit for light duty, not that it meant anything.

The one KIA was Corporal Edgar Jerousek, Jr., a motor pool mechanic. No one knew him well. He was a loner. He spent most of his days under a truck or working on one of the tracked vehicles. He never quit working until after sunset when it was too dark to work. Then he would go to the club covered in black grease and smelling of motor oil. He always sat by himself and drank two cans of beer before taking his shower in solitude. That was the last shower he would take.

Sneed gathered Jerousek's few personal items and gave them to the division recovery team which packed what was left of him into a body bag. His 782 gear was returned to supply. All traces of Corporal Edgar Jerousek, Jr. were gone by zero nine hundred hours.

CHAPTER 23

September 1966
I Corps – Indian Country

Vietnam War Timeline: The U.S. revealed that jungles near the DMZ are being defoliated by sprayed chemicals. The chemical that became best known was referred to as Agent Orange because the canisters in which it was stored were marked with an orange band.

The monsoon season would be starting in October. The I-Corps area expected to receive over 100 inches of rain in a four-month period. That meant that any major movements needed to occur before the rains came.

In late August First 8" Inch Howitzer Battery was ordered north to support the increased fighting with the NVA that was occurring in Thua Thien Province, referred to as Indian Country.

Briggs' first view of the new TAOR (Tactical Area of Responsibility) was on a brilliant clear day. He and Bo stood on a high point that allowed them to see the South China Sea off to his right and an unhindered view of the coastal plains for at least 20 miles west to the hill country.

The scene was marred by puffs of smoke in the distance from 105 mm howitzer shells exploding. They were too far away to hear the artillery or small arms fire. The land spoke of death. Briggs thought of General George Custer viewing the battlefield at Little Bighorn before his troops were massacred by the Sioux Indians ninety years before. It crossed his mind that they could suffer a similar fate. That's why they called it Indian Country.

The move was conducted over a three-day period. It was all hands-on deck. Orders for two Marines to go on R&R were canceled. They were already on a truck headed to Danang to catch their flight to Taipei when they were ordered to return.

Work parties were conducted 24 / 7 packing up equipment, ammunition, food, supplies, weapons, communication equipment, cots, tables - everything that supported life for a 180-man combat unit living in a primitive and self-supporting environment.

Having been in the same location for seven months, there was a lot of non-essential items that had been collected that would not be making the move. It was like cleaning out a closet at home. A giant bonfire was kept burning during the entire moving period.

Lance Corporal Worsham was a dog lover. He had adopted two strays for pets. They were named after Marine Corps heroes, Chesty (Puller) and Smedley (Butler). Worsham picked up after the dogs. He fed them mess hall leftovers. They stuck close to him. Where he went, they went. When he was on duty the dogs stayed in a pen he built for them under his hooch.

At night they hung out at the enlisted club until Worsham discovered someone had filled their water dish with beer. It doesn't take much to get a dog drunk. Both Chesty and Smedley staggered around until they passed out.

Everyone agreed that having the dogs around provided a touch of home. They hadn't caused any problems. They became beloved pets. But when the move was announced it was their death sentence. They could not go along, and they would not survive being left behind.

First Sergeant Callahan delivered the bad news to Worsham. Like a lawyer trying to keep his client off death row, Worsham passionately argued their case. Chesty and Smedley were each executed with a bullet to the head. Their bodies were cremated in the bonfire. Worsham remained angry and bitter the rest of his tour.

It was rumored that an Army unit was taking over Firebase Diamond, so no one was about to leave too much behind other than the command and guard posts, sandbagged bunkers and concertina wire. The showers rebuilt by the Seabees after the mortar attack also survived demolition.

The most dangerous part of the move would be splitting the force in three as it moved 40 miles north. An advance group was assigned with setting up the new base. It had been used briefly by two infantry companies from the Ninth Marines. All that was left behind were a couple of hoochs, fighting holes and sandbags. New positions would have to be cleared for the howitzers, ammo dump and command post. Marine engineers with bulldozers were called upon to help with that job.

One group would be in transit with no guarantee they would reach a fortified base before nightfall. If not, then they had to call in their position, circle the wagons and stay on hundred percent alert all night.

A final group was left behind to fare for itself for two nights. Everyone had to operate short-handed. This is when they were most vulnerable.

On day one the mess hall, the clubs and a couple of the sleeping hooches were dismantled. The lumber, aluminum roof and canvas tarps were loaded on trucks scheduled to head out at first light on day two. Three 8" howitzers were sent ahead to begin support operations.

The 26-ton self-propelled howitzers were too heavy for the ancient bridge across the murky Cu De River. They had to be floated across on a barge. The engineers oversaw the operation which took about two hours for each weapon to be loaded, floated and unloaded.

It was a dicey maneuver fraught with things that could go wrong. After successfully moving two howitzers across the river, something did go wrong.

The last howitzer, with its name "Howlin' Mad" painted on the barrel, was being driven onto the barge when it broke away from its shore ties and violently pushed into the river. The howitzer was left dangling off the lip. Its weight lifted the front of the barge into the air. The driver gunned the motor trying desperately to gain traction and balance.

The giant motor raced at maximum RPMs. The tracked wheels ground into the wooden barge. It only took about 10 seconds for gravity to suck "Howlin' Mad," and its crew under the water with an immense splash sending waves 20 feet high. The barge, with its cargo off lifted, shot into the air and then crashed into the river like a surfboard that had lost its rider.

The driver was trapped inside the tank. There was no getting out. Two other crew members were on top outside. One was thrown backwards onto the land. He was the only one to survive despite a broken neck. The other was thrown into the river where he was sucked under the tank.

Both supervising engineers on the barge were killed. One of them was seen bouncing violently off the metal tank before disappearing into the water. The other was thrown as if by a sling shot, 30 yards downriver.

Bo and Briggs had witnessed the earlier crossings. Everything seemed to be going to plan and Bo wanted to get back to Firebase Diamond to make sure cleanup was continuing there. They were seven miles away when the radio call came.

"Holy fuck," was the only response Bo could muster when he was told what had happened. Briggs turned the jeep around and headed back. Their only conversation during this time was Bo muttering: "I'm fucked. I'm fucked."

Briggs figured Bo was more worried that this was a career ender for him rather than concern for the dead crewmen. Four dead. One seriously injured. He was the CO. He was responsible. The fact that he couldn't be in two places at the same time did not mean anything in the big scheme of things. It happened on his watch.

A week later, it took two giant tracked vehicles to pull the sunken howitzer out of the water. It was hauled off to be reconditioned and would eventually be re-entered into service. "Howlin' Mad" lived to shoot again.

The bodies were recovered and slipped into bags for shipment home. The one crewman who survived was flown to the military hospital at Clark Air Force Base in the Philippines. His war was over.

There is no time for grieving and solace. A week after the accident, Father Fred Lucky, a Catholic priest and career military chaplain, arrived from division headquarters to conduct a field memorial service. Father Fred was also known as Sweaty Freddy, because his uniform arm pits were always stained from perspiration.

Sweaty Freddy had been busy lately holding similar services throughout I-Corps. He was able to conduct a moving service in less than a half hour. Anyone not on guard duty or radio watch was required to attend. Fortunately, there were no fire missions called in while the service was being conducted so the big guns remained silent.

Bo knew it was only a matter of time before he would be relieved. Most field grade officers were getting new assignments about every four months. Since he had already been in country with the battery more than eight months, he was overdue for rotation. He hoped that would be the reason stated in his personnel file for his transfer rather than the incident at the Cu De River.

Firebase Diamond was no more. That name stayed behind. The battery was now operating out of Firebase Chippewa. Firebases throughout I-Corps were named after other warlike Indian tribes such as Firebase Apache and Firebase Iroquois.

Briggs and Sneed, over a few beers, agreed that Firebase Chippewa sounded more like a summer camp than a lethal artillery firing base.

Bo was around long enough to participate in one last event, the recognition of the 100,000th round fired by the 12th Marine regiment in Vietnam. Most of the rounds fired were by the workhorse 105 mm howitzers which were lighter and easier to relocate as needed. Battery B, First Battalion, 12th Marines, claimed to have fired over 15,000 rounds. They received recognition for the most rounds fired.

The 8" howitzer fired a 203-pound shell, the Big Bertha as it was known, so it was chosen for firing the celebratory round. It made for a better photo op than the smaller 105s.

A media event was hosted by General Walt and his command staff. Photographers and reporters were ferried out to Firebase Chippewa in a CH-47 Chinook helicopter. A Big Bertha was decorated with the Marine Corps and regimental logos and inscribed in yellow paint with "100,000 rounds."

Photographers were snapping pictures as the round was loaded and General Walt made the obligatory remarks about how the war was being won through the hard work, dedication and teamwork of the American and South Vietnamese allies.

On General Walt's signal, Bo had the honor of pulling the lanyard launching the round which was aimed at a pre-selected target deep in Indian Country. The media guests, most who were not used to the sound of a howitzer of this size firing so close, were obviously startled. A few of them instinctively ducked for cover thinking it was incoming.

The next day, Bo received his orders and was on a chopper out of Firebase Chippewa by 0900 hours. Captain Mains became the acting CO until another major could be found to fill the billet.

CHAPTER 24

October 1966
I Corps – Indian Country

Vietnam War Timeline: President Lyndon B. Johnson made a surprise visit to Vietnam to meet with troops and solemnly pledge to them "we shall never let you down nor your fighting comrades." He spent two hours and 24 minutes at the well-protected Cam Rahn Bay supply base.

The rains started slowly in mid-October. A couple gloomy days with scattered showers and thunderstorms were followed by partially sunny days that seemed to contradict the predictions of the severe monsoons to follow.

There was a noticeable drop in nighttime temperatures. Weapons needed to be cleaned every day because of the increased humidity. Briggs panicked after not looking at his M-14 for three days to discover enough orange that he could have been court martialed.

Even though he had kept his rifle wrapped in an extra blanket it wasn't enough to ward off the rust in any spot where the rifle had been nicked and unprotected from the elements. From then on, he checked it twice a day.

Briggs got his sergeant stripes in an impromptu promotion ceremony on October 16, four years and 3 months to the day after his original enlistment date. When he first entered the Marine Corps, it was rare that a sergeant had less than eight years in service time. During a war promotion came quickly.

The ceremony was held in the large tent that served as the enlisted club which could provide cover from the rain for 40 troops squeezed in back to back. There were six other promotions celebrated that day. Briggs and Sneed both made sergeant. With all the administrative magic that Sneed was able to make happen, Briggs wondered if Sneed hadn't promoted himself.

Also being promoted were two new lance corporals and one new corporal. Sergeant Latham became a staff sergeant and 2nd Lieutenant Al Burns got his silver 1st LT bars.

Gunny Lincoln did the honors for Briggs. He pinned on the black metal collar insignia, 3 stripes over crossed rifles, and gave him an extra firm handshake. "Congratulations sergeant."

"Thanks Gunny." Nothing else needed to be said. The two men shared a personal bond that communicated their feelings to each other. Briggs could feel the pride Lincoln had in him. Briggs never wanted to disappoint the older man who had become his mentor.

By the end of the month, the monsoons had arrived. Once or twice a day the rain would let up for an hour in the morning, but it ranged from a steady shower to a downpour during mid-afternoon through the night. The world was like a black and white movie with the colors replaced by a gray sky and green landscape.

The pace of the war seemed to match the weather. It was difficult to know what progress was being made. Technically, the 1st 8" Howitzer Battery was supporting Operation Pawnee, a three-month search and destroy mission aimed at extracting the VC and NVA from Thua Thien Province.

They also provided cover fire for smaller daily and weekly ops conducted by the Marines and ARVN such as Operation Craddock, Operation Dover and Operation Madison. Briggs wondered if there was an entire unit devoted to thinking up names. He was never sure who was on the other end of the radio or which operation got which fire mission.

When Briggs made sergeant, he was relieved of driving for Captain Mains. He was needed supervising the radio squad. His world became a small circle trudging through mud from his sleeping hooch to the radio shack to the mess hall and to the fire direction center bunker to stand radio watches.

There was a constant rotation of radio operators being assigned to infantry units as forward observers, tough dangerous duty. Some of them never returned. The lucky ones rotated out when their tours ended. The casualty rate was high among FOs. Word would circle back when one of their own was among those evacuated dead or alive.

The remainder of the squad at call sign Ringo One operated short-handed. Radio watches were extended and often doubled. That was okay with Briggs. He liked to do two shifts, eight hours overnight and then sleep in the next day avoiding work parties and patrols.

Not too many fire missions were called in at night since the FOs couldn't see their targets. They were hunkered down in an observation post, underneath a poncho. Staying dry was not an option. Radio checks were required every half hour to make sure they were still alive, and the batteries retained some juice.

Communication from the FO was often with nothing more than the click of the handset. That indicated he was in the shit and didn't feel safe to voice answer. Pre-sighted target coordinates for the big guns were called in before nightfall each day in case of an enemy attack. Some targets were as close as 300 yards from friendly forces.

Sitting radio watches in the command bunker seemed like routine office work. Two radio operators sitting across a wide table faced each other. Their job was to help blow up people, buildings, and machines.

Each was responsible for monitoring two PRC-25s giving them coverage of four different radio nets. Speaker boxes were modulated to hold down the constant static that was interrupted by routine radio traffic from the battalion and regimental nets. The FOs stayed silent until it was shooting time.

Briggs liked working with the newly promoted 1st Lieutenant Al Burns. Being a junior officer, Burns often caught the overnight shift in the fire control center. He was 23 years old, an ROTC graduate from Indiana State University fulfilling his active duty commitment. He had blue eyes, light brown hair, stood over six feet tall with an athletic build. Briggs thought Burns would make a great recruiting poster Marine.

Being a one-and-done officer, he planned to go to law school after completing his hitch. He had a relaxed working relationship with the enlisted men that was different from the career officers. Both being from the Midwest he and Briggs often passed the slow hours of the night by talking about Big Ten football and basketball.

Burns was, nevertheless, serious about the business of killing the enemy by figuring out how to drop large explosives on them from miles away. He was a graduate of the Army Artillery School at Fort Hood, Texas.

Briggs viewed the field artillery team as a hands-off system of organized mayhem. He was impressed at how quickly they could drop the chit chat and turn to the task of killing nameless, faceless enemy soldiers or the innocent civilian who accidentally happened to be in the range an exploding Big Bertha.

When Briggs received the request for a fire mission from the FO, he verbally announced it so everyone in the bunker could hear.

"Sir, fire mission from FO Sauce Three-Five."

They all jumped into action. Everyone had a role to play.

"Target. Enemy concentration. Men and trucks."

Everything was repeated between Briggs and the FO.

"Coordinates – 8-4-3-7 4-4-1-5. I repeat 8-4-3-7 4-4-1-5." Briggs was talking to the FO and everyone in the FDC at the same time. Getting the coordinates right was the most important element of a fire mission.

"Two rounds. Hotel Echo. Will adjust."

"Roger. Two rounds. H E. Will adjust," Briggs repeated. H E was short for High Explosive, meant to break bunkers and shower infantry with shrapnel.

Briggs quickly scribbled details on a pre-printed fire mission order form and signed his name to it. There was a point of responsibility for everyone in the killing chain. There needed to be a paper trail in case a mistake occurred, and someone needed to have their ass chewed or court martialed.

Working at a plotting board using a T-Square, a triangle and a compass to calculate elevation, range and trajectory, Burns could have been designing an office building or a bridge. It required just as much skill and precision. The shells would hit a target miles away with some geometry and a few mathematical equations.

The team consisted of the FO, the radio operator, the fire control supervisor, and the gun crew. They were all guilty of conspiracy to murder.

After details of the mission were confirmed and reconfirmed, the FO calmly stated, "fire when ready." Everyone in the FDC heard it over the loudspeaker. Briggs was still required to relay the order verbally.

"Fire when ready." Lt. Burns repeated the order to Lance Corporal Louie Tellish who was on the land line to the gun crews. Burns had decided to use two howitzers to complete the mission.

It had taken less than two minutes from the time the FO had first called in his mission until Briggs reported "On the way."

The FDC team waited silently for a response from the FO. It seemed to them to take forever. Burns even gave Briggs a nod to do a radio check when suddenly the FO was back: "Ringo One this is Sauce Three -Five. Adjust one hundred right, fifty up. Fire for effect."

Briggs repeated the instructions to Burns who did a quick re-calculation then gave Tellish the new gun settings. Within one minute the big guns boomed again. "Fire for effect" were the magic words that unleashed the ultimate destructive power of the howitzers.

None of the FDC team would ever see the explosions or the chunks of steel shrapnel that would tear apart a Vietnamese teenager. When the FO reported back "Cease Fire. Six KIA," they celebrated like a football team after scoring a touchdown.

Five minutes after the mission concluded it was if it had never happened. The men in the FDC returned to waiting. They lit up cigarettes and drank stale coffee from a thermos. Some men not on duty claimed they could sleep through the bombardment. It was just another fire mission. Those on guard duty kept staring out at their field of fire.

The gray, dreary November weather began to wear on people. They drank more. Some drugs were being brought onto the firebase. There seemed to be more petty arguments and morale was in a slow decline.

In the radio squad PFC Whitman, the draftee, "college boy," became more bitter, sullen, and uncooperative. When he did interact with anyone he was patronizing and condescending. His smirk was particularly irritating. Because of the dampness, equipment maintenance had become a full-time job. Briggs had to watch Whitman constantly to make sure he did what he was supposed to do. Everything with Whitman was met with push back.

It came to a head one night when Whitman was scheduled to relieve Briggs on radio watch at 0200 hours. Twice Briggs had to roust him out of his rack.

On his third trip to Whitman's hooch, Briggs flipped his cot over. He crashed onto the plywood floor like Sonny Liston taking a right cross from Cassius Clay.

"What the fuck?" Whitman jumped up with fists cocked. Briggs was ready for the punch he was sure would come his way.

"Take a swing ass wipe. You'll spend the rest of your time here in jail," Briggs said. The two men stood motionless each waiting for the other to make the next move. They stared each other down in the dark.

Briggs was ready to kick his ass if necessary, but he was sure Whitman would not swing. He was an asshole, but he wasn't dumb.

"You're a half hour late. Get dressed and get your ass over to the FDC," Briggs ordered. "Now!"

When Whitman finally showed up, the shift change was executed without any words being spoken.

CHAPTER 25

November 1966
Thua Thien Province

Vietnam War Timeline: U.S. military personnel lost during November was 666. Their names were inscribed on panel 12E of the Vietnam Wall.

When not working, the social structure was awkward for the newly appointed sergeant E-5s. They weren't invited to drink with the officers and senior NCO's who had their own club. They had no choice but to continue spending their off hours with the enlisted ranks.

Briggs recalled similar experiences when he was promoted to corporal at Camp Lejeune. He was no longer allowed entrance into the EM Club. His friendships with those of lower ranks slowly melted away. It was the general order of things in the military. It would take longer this time because they still drank together under the same tent, but he would have no choice but to begin to separate himself.

The football "Game of the Century" (one of many) was played in East Lansing, Michigan, on Saturday afternoon, November 19. Michigan State versus Notre Dame. The two best teams in the country. In Vietnam, it was early Sunday morning,

The football game was broadcast live on Armed Forces radio. The two teams were ranked nationally 1 and 2, both undefeated. Even though they were waging a daily war 10,000 miles away, the men at Firebase Chippewa had intense interest in the game. It was a reminder that life as they knew it went on at home.

Briggs was on radio watch that night. Other than the regular radio checks and the scheduled H&I fire missions, it was a slow night.

A small transistor radio was tuned to the game. Lieutenant Burns was on duty in the FDC with Briggs. Burns cheered for Notre Dame. Briggs for Michigan State. There was a lot of good-natured ribbing as the game started out in MSU's favor but then the momentum swung to the Irish. The game ended in a 10 -10 tie, leaving the question of which was the best team to be debated endlessly.

November was a gray, wet month that provided little relief. It was the small events like listening to the game that provided a break. Thanksgiving followed. The cooks prepared a traditional meal of turkey, dressing and mashed potatoes. Of course, everything was supplied in cans, so it wasn't like mom's home cooking. But it was a welcome change from the usual daily menus of creamed beef on toast or other mystery meat.

There was little grumbling because artillery knew they had it better than the grunts who were eating C-Rations every meal, every day underneath a poncho in Indian Country.

The battery was supporting multiple operations: Operation Prairie One, Operation Arcadia, Operation Rio Grande. No one ever knew the final outcomes. This was not football. No scores were posted. There was usually some brief coverage on each operation in the daily issue of the Stars & Stripes newspaper. They made it sound like the U.S. won every battle and the VC and NVA were always on the run.

Between the big guns at Firebase Chippewa and those that were deployed to the various infantry battalions, the battery was able to support operations from the South China Sea on the east to the border of Laos on the west.

Captain Mains had moved on to another assignment more in line with his rank and experience. He had made no impression on anyone during his relatively short time as CO after Bo left. The troops referred to him as "Mad Dog" Mains, but that was more of a sarcastic comment on his lack of personality than due to his command presence.

"Mad Dog" was most remembered for the day that he accidentally discharged his weapon while cleaning it, blowing a hole in the roof of his hooch. The hole was patched with a piece of canvas held in place by glue and duct tape. The troops enjoyed the fact that it always leaked. Served him right. He had pissed everyone off when he confiscated a combat shotgun that was meant to be used on patrols. Mad Dog never went on any patrols.

Major Benjamin A. Cavalo, a career officer and ROTC graduate from the University of Maine, was the new CO. A short transfer of command ceremony was held in the EM club tent.

Major Cavalo had been serving in division headquarters waiting for a command since he arrived in country in July. When a new commander takes over there is a sense that he needs to make his presence felt. That would include an immediate review of the firebase defense, enhanced equipment maintenance, announcements about uniform regulations and daily procedures. None of these things were bad, it was simply different. The major concern was hoping that Cavalo would not enforce the daily quota of two beers a day.

Cavalo handled it all in a steady, but low-key manner. He and Gunny Lincoln spent three days walking the perimeter of the firebase, inside the wire and out. Other officers and NCOs joined them when requested. A few guard posts were moved, and others added, adjusting and creating new fields of fire. The ammo dump became multiple ammo dumps. The big guns received additional protection which meant more sandbags to be filled. He did not rustle anyone's feathers, but it was clear that a new sheriff was in town.

It was critical to maintain troop morale during the monsoon season when doom and gloom was omnipresent. Cavalo took time to shake hands with every man asking about his family and hometown. He discussed the importance of their military jobs. He would ask how much time they had in country but never asked how much time they had left. He did not want to be creating any short timer attitudes.

Briggs and Sneed met most days about 1600 hours at the club to down a couple of beers before evening chow. Occasionally they would exceed their official military quota of two beers per man per day. Most men had extra beer or liquor stashed in their hooch. The longer the monsoon season lasted the more drinking they did.

"What's your read on the old man," Briggs asked.

"So far, so good. I like the way he goes about things. He's not all riled up. More of a steady as you go type. I don't think much is going to get past him. He's got Gunny Lincoln on his side. That's a big plus."

"The question is how long will we have this guy? It seems to me that all the lifers are over here getting their tickets punched. Bo came over with the unit and stayed, what, eight months? That's a lifetime. We won't see that again," Briggs commented.

"I see the orders for all the incoming and outgoing officers in the regiment. It's a continual flow at that field grade level. Those are the guys who have to make it now or get out and find a civilian job," Sneed explained.

"What R&R billets are coming in these days," Briggs asked. He had passed his halfway tour hump day and was thinking about putting in his request. He wasn't sure where he wanted to go. Hong Kong was the front runner on his short list.

"They just opened up Hawaii. I'm sure all the married officers are going to snatch up that trip. Lance corporal shit bird married to Buffy back home has about as much chance of seeing Waikiki as a fart in a windstorm."

Sneed was the man in the know on all things at headquarters. The Rest & Recuperation trips provided five days' vacation from the war. First 8" Howitzer Battery had not seen any R&R during its first six months in country. Once the Marine Corps settled in for the long haul, the weekly postings became more important than the daily mail or happy hour.

R&R was informally known as I&I, "intoxication and intercourse." Each unit was given a set percentage of billets based on their manpower numbers. Eligibility was granted based on seniority and availability. Gunny Lincoln and First Sergeant Callahan ultimately decided who got to go. It paid not to be on their wrong side.

"Most everything I've seen coming through lately has been for Taipei or Manila. There have been a couple for Bangkok. I'm hearing good things about Thailand. I think there are some new places opening. Of course, all anyone is looking for is five days of pussy. Over here it all goes sideways."

Sneed promised Briggs he would keep an eye out for Hong Kong and let him know when it was available. It paid to get advance information.

The most popular topic of discussion when someone returned from R&R was about the bar girls. An entire Asian sex industry had been created to serve American GIs. A prostitute could be rented for $10 a day to be a companion, guide and sex partner.

Asian cities were also a marketplace for cheap electronics, jewelry and clothing. The American dollar had a lot of buying power.

On his R&R to Taipei, PFC Larry Canonica had purchased an eight-track, reel to reel tape recorder for half the price he would pay in the states. He made recordings of him having sex with his bar girl, Lucy. The two of them were noisy lovemakers. For a few weeks Canonica's hooch was a popular hangout as he played the pornographic recording upon request. Canonica served on one of the gun crews. He was considered a weird dude. His primary physical features were bad teeth and a homemade tattoo on his left forearm that read "MOM" from his viewpoint and "WOW" for everyone else.

Briggs had radio watch that night, so he wanted to limit his drinking. They slogged their way over to the mess tent a little after 1700 hours. They carried their tin mess kits with them. Seating was on picnic table benches provided courtesy of the Seabees.

Sergeant Hong, the Vietnamese interrogator / translator assigned to the battery always sat by himself. No one tried to get to know him. No one knew what he did. Since they were not capturing any prisoners there weren't any to interrogate. Hong would spend a few nights with the battery then be gone for a week or more.

He was enlisted but because of his status as a foreign soldier, he had a cot in a tent with three officers. He was always well groomed wearing a silk ascot with uniforms that looked brand new. He used lots of cologne. You knew he was heading your way if you were 10 feet downwind.

"You think he's VC?" Briggs asked.

"You ask me that every time we talk about him. He never seems to be here when we get shot at. I'm suspicious that he knows when the shit is about to hit the fan. But he seems to like all things American, particularly round-eye women with big breasts. He's got a great porn collection."

"Playboy pinups?" Briggs asked.

"No. That's too mild for him. He likes the French shit. Really raunchy. Hard core."

"Maybe we ought to get to know him better."

"What? Invite him over to have dinner with us? No fucking way. I don't want to talk to that guy," Sneed responded. "Let's just wait until he gets blown away and then we can sneak into his tent and steal his porn."

There was a high level of suspicion of all the Vietnamese. The base relied on locals for haircuts, trash hauling and laundry service. Three teenaged girls assisted the cooks in return for meals and a small stipend that was paid in Vietnamese Dong, the funny money that looked like it was printed on carbon paper.

"Speaking of pussy, how's the girl back in the states?" Sneed asked.

"I'm sure she's shopping for my Christmas present as we speak," Briggs replied sarcastically. "I think she's gone on with her life without me. And, of course, I've gone on with mine. Who do you think is enjoying their life more, her or me?"

"Oh you, of course. You are here fighting for truth, justice and the American way. You are keeping America safe from the commie menace." Briggs and Sneed laughed at their shared misery. Briggs felt the pain of loss as he thought about Brenda. His 23rd birthday passed two weeks before without hearing from Brenda.

They sanitized their mess kits in the barrels of boiling water and headed off to their respective hooch. Briggs had radio watch at 2200 hours. He would try to get a couple hours sleep before heading back to the FDC.

CHAPTER 26

December 1966
Thua Thien Province

Vietnam War Timeline: As the year ended, there were 385,000 U.S. troops in country. Americans killed in action was 6,644. The South Vietnam Armed Forces totaled 735,000 men in uniform.

"How many forts do you figure the fucking French built over here? Seems to me there's one around every corner," Briggs commented. He pointed to the ruins on the nearby hilltop.

"Yeah, I know. Kind of a shitload isn't it," Gunny Lincoln answered. "Well the frogs were here since the last century, so I suppose they had plenty of time to build things. But it looks like a pretty static way to fight a war. They were probably Foreign Legion."

Briggs was driving Gunny Lincoln to check out possible sites where one or two howitzers could be placed to support another operation that was expected to launch within the next month. It would give them shooting access to the southwest toward the Laotian border. As the Marines had moved north, intelligence reports confirmed that NVA troops had circled around them entering Vietnam from that direction.

This was normally the job of Major Cavalo or the XO. But the major had been called to a meeting of all the artillery top brass at division head-quarters with I-Corps Commanding General Lew Walt. When Cavalo was off base, the XO was required to stay aboard.

After 42 days of rain, there had been a break in the weather. The sun had even peaked out on a few occasions. The amount of U.S. military vehicles, private cars, trucks, and busses on the main paved roads was like rush hour traffic. The dirt roads had firmed up as the rains slowed.

Gunny Lincoln volunteered to investigate the sites that division planners had already marked on their maps as prospective firing support locations. He rarely had been off Firebase Chippewa since the move and was getting antsy. He chose Briggs to be his driver.

They had followed the map along unnamed roads that led through hamlets and between rice paddies. After passing a marine guard post a couple klicks back, they no longer saw any other military traffic. Briggs began to wonder if they should be out this far roaming around by themselves.

"Let's take a ride up the hill and take a look," Lincoln said. "I've been wondering about those old forts ever since I got here. Plus, we might get a good view from up there. See if we can pinpoint some firing sites."

The remains of the fort were one of many fortifications that the French had left behind when they abandoned Vietnam in 1954. They were constructed of cement, bricks and rock. They were meant to be permanent, unlike the U.S. which built bases of plywood and canvas that could go up quickly and be torn down just as fast. It didn't seem as if the U.S. was planning on being here for the long term. The French had viewed Vietnam as one of their colonies. The U.S. viewed it as a place to block communism. Both countries underestimated what it took to accomplish their goals.

The outlines of an old road wound its way gradually up to the hilltop which sat about 100 feet above the surrounding terrain. The jeep slipped a bit on the long, wet grass and mud until the deep tread of the tires grabbed hold. The verdant green countryside revealed itself until it disappeared into a mist several miles away.

"This would be a great place for a house," Gunny commented.

"Yeah. If you didn't have to live here," Briggs responded. He parked the jeep between the remains of two walls made of what appeared to be a natural black rock held together with mortar.

The fort had been built on a tabletop rather than a peak. The sides of the hill didn't begin to drop off for a few hundred yards. A thick stand of trees dominated one side where the terrain dipped towards the flooded rice paddies below.

The level of deterioration indicated the fort had been constructed well before World War II. They walked around a pile of old timbers which had been part of a roof. There was one room still standing. Briggs poked his head in long enough to get a whiff of something wet and putrid. He decided it didn't need any more investigation.

Gunny Lincoln scanned the horizon with his binoculars looking for potential firebase sites. He was checking what he saw against the map that they had been provided by the regimental S-3 office.

The problem, of course, was that officers in S-3 never went in the field. They looked at brightly colored maps and without knowing what the terrain was like, they marked where they thought things should be located. The map didn't always match up with reality.

"See anything out there Gunny," Briggs asked.

"Nothing but a lot of shit filled rice paddies," he answered. "This is farm country. The breadbasket of Vietnam." Briggs understood Gunny's mismatched midwestern U.S. metaphor. They could see farmers working the paddies with their water buffalos.

After a few minutes of poking around the rubble, they sat down on a flat portion of one of the walls that was still standing to enjoy the view. Gunny lit a cigarette. He was always trying to quit smoking but gave himself the luxury of a daily quota. He savored each cigarette as if it were his last. He wouldn't have another for at least three hours.

They talked for a few minutes about what it must have been like for the French garrison to be stationed here. Neither of them knew much about Vietnamese history. They could, however, recognize the signs of French influence throughout the area. Many of the private cars they saw on the roads were identified by their distinctive swoop back as French-made Citroen. The drivers and their passengers were often Caucasians. Many buildings in Danang exhibited the influence of French architecture. Road signs and billboards were often expressed in both Vietnamese and French.

Out of the corner of his eye, Briggs became aware that there was movement coming from the tree line one hundred yards behind them.

"Holy shit gunny. We got company," Briggs said.

There were six Vietnamese, all dressed in black pajamas walking towards them at a fast pace. They carried rifles. This wasn't a welcoming committee. They were VC. Game on.

"Let's get the fuck out of here," Gunny Lincoln said. They sprinted for their Jeep 20 yards away where they had carelessly left their M-14s just not thinking they were needed.

When they started running, the VC did the same. They began shouting. A couple shots were fired.

Briggs jumped behind the wheel, pressed the start button and slammed the shift into reverse. He had a strange moment of clarity as he cursed himself for not having parked the jeep pointed in the direction of easy escape.

Gunny Lincoln almost fell out of the Jeep as Briggs braked and then threw it into forward gear. The gunny grabbed his rifle and tried to get into a position to return fire as more shots were fired. At least two of them hit the Jeep body. Another skipped by on the ground. Lincoln had all he could do to stay in the Jeep as Briggs headed down the bumpy access road at a speed that would not be considered safe.

Briggs suddenly felt a hot stinging sensation in his left leg. It caused him to involuntarily jump but he was able to keep his attention on the road.

His only response to the wound was to yell "Shit!"

Briggs was aware that Gunny Lincoln had got a couple shots off but figured that it was doubtful he would hit anything bouncing around the way they were.

More shots were fired at them as they descended toward the road below. One round found the windshield shattering the glass into a spider web that required Briggs to lean out the Jeep door to see where he was going.

As they reached the road the firing stopped. Briggs looked at the speedometer. He was going 60 kph on a road made for 25 kph. He didn't slow down for another two minutes until he was sure they were out of range.

Briggs slammed on the brakes, throwing Gunny Lincoln awkwardly into the dashboard. Fortunately, he had braced himself, his arms absorbing the collision. Using his rifle butt, Briggs smashed out the windshield so he could see. He glanced down at his bloody calf. The blood was not gushing so he knew it hadn't hit any main artery.

Briggs drove at a more normal speed towards Firebase Chippewa. Other than a lot of deep breathing neither of them had spoken a word.

Gunny Lincoln finally broke the tense silence between them. "Well, that sure as hell made for an exciting day. You okay? How's your leg?"

"It feels like a through and through. I think it took a chunk out of the back of my calf. I feel a hole back there. Hurts like a son of a bitch. I'll live. How about you?"

"I'm still checking to see if all my parts are still with me. I think so. I'm more worried about having a heart attack," the Gunny said.

"I guess that qualifies as being in a firefight. Right?"

"Yep. First and hopefully last one. And you got yourself a purple heart."

"Yeah. Just what I always wanted," Briggs commented through gritted teeth. His leg felt like someone was holding a flame to it. He had always wondered what it felt like to get shot.

"Nice driving. You should think about running at the Indy 500. If we hadn't gotten out of there, we were headed for a long stay in some jungle hotel. We were trophy bait."

Back at base Briggs got patched up by Doc Flores, the battery corpsman. It was considered a flesh wound. He checked Gunny Lincoln's blood pressure and gave him a couple of aspirin and a pat on the back.

Gunny Lincoln reported into Major Cavalo who was back from his meeting. He was required to write an after-action report. He recommended that future site trips be comprised of a fully armed squad and multiple vehicles.

Briggs ended up on light duty for a couple weeks. He was given a crutch to help him walk although he found it virtually useless in the soft ground around the base. It was easier to slide his leg along. He still sat radio watches and spent time in the comm tent helping with maintenance while sitting on a camp stool.

CHAPTER 27

Christmas 1966
Thua Thien Province

Vietnam War Timeline: 1966 - The U.S. Selective Service drafted 382,010 men into service. The last KIA of the year was Corporal Gary G. Schneider, 19, L Company, 3rd Battalion, 26th Marines. Total U.S. killed during the year exceeded 6,000.

Briggs was officially on light duty. That just meant he did not have to go on any work parties or patrols. He still had to handle his radio watches. He spent a lot of time sitting on a stool in the comm shack supervising equipment maintenance and shooting the shit with the platoon.

Twice he had to make trips to Med Central, near division headquarters to get his wounds redressed and have a doctor evaluate his healing process. Doc Flores had done a good job of dressing the initial battlefield wound. Driving the sick and lame to Med Central once a week was the responsibility of PFC Risdon who still served as the house mouse despite the changes in commanding officers.

Med Central was a constantly growing and evolving medical hub of tents and hastily constructed buildings that housed the I-Corps primary emergency lifesaving facility and surgery unit. Incoming helicopters buzzed in and out 24/7, with wounded troops from the battlefield whose care always took priority.

Briggs never minded the delays. The longer he got to hang around waiting for treatment the more he got to watch the American female nurses, the round eyes. Regardless of age, size or personality, they all looked attractive to him.

It was usually a female nurse who redressed his wound. A doctor would take a quick look and sign off on some report attached to a clip board. It never took more than 15 minutes. The nurses kept conversation to a minimum. No sense in encouraging sex deprived Marines who wanted to fall in love.

The waiting area was not designed for comfort. No one expected anything more than a hard bench and access to the smoking area. The dental unit was located around the corner. There being no sound absorption Briggs could hear the drills grinding. He had once spent a couple hours there himself when he had two impacted wisdom teeth removed. It took him almost three weeks before he could chew. He existed on soft stuff that he could shove between his swollen jaws.

The only reading material offered were a few back issues of Stars & Stripes, Leatherneck Magazine and Marine Corps Gazette. An occasional copy of Time Magazine or Sports Illustrated would show up, only to soon disappear.

Each visit consumed at least a half day, most of that time spent waiting for treatment. Risdon sometimes made two round trips each day. He didn't wait around if he was needed back at base.

Sometimes he would also drop off the walking wounded at the Main PX which grew each day with more American made products. There was an attempt to decorate the giant warehouse with a sparsely decorated plastic Christmas tree, some sparkly lights, and a faux Santa Claus. No one seemed to care. This was a war zone.

Mounds of Christmas candy had made its way across the ocean. The presence of some items seemed to make no sense but were considered a luxury to troops in the field. Briggs bought two quarts of dill pickles. They were a popular item at Firebase Chippewa.

Navy Ensign Roger Staubach, the Heisman Trophy winner from the U.S. Naval Academy was seen cruising the aisles at the PX. He was serving his naval commitment at a supply and petroleum depot near Danang. Celebrity sightings were a big deal.

On his second trip to Med Central, Briggs ran into Corporal Nick Forhan. They knew each other from training at Camp Pendleton before being shipped overseas. Forhan was a former iron mill worker from Massachusetts. He had a strong, lanky build and from what Briggs had seen at Pendleton, appeared to have amazing stamina. He was always the first to the top of Pendleton's challenging hills, or what some people would describe as small mountains. He could walk all day with a 40-pound backpack.

He was now serving as a squad leader in Bravo Company, 1st battalion, 9th Marines and had recently taken some shrapnel from a grenade. He didn't know if it was from friendly fire or the bad guys.

Briggs felt he had drawn a lucky straw going to artillery. It was safer duty than being a grunt. But that didn't keep him from feeling envy and admiration for infantry warriors like Forhan.

They stepped outside so Forhan could have a smoke. "Have you seen some shit?" Briggs asked.

"Yeah. It hasn't been pretty. I'm just trying to get home in one piece. This is my second purple heart. One more and they put me on the big bird back to the states."

"What was the first one," Briggs asked.

"I stepped on a punji stake. It went completely through my foot. It hurt like hell. Much worse than the shrapnel wound. My leg ballooned up right away from the water boo shit or whatever they put on those things. My squad had to carry me back to base. I had a world class infection. I was sick as shit for about two weeks. "Technically, stepping on a punji stake isn't purple heart qualified, but the Doc wrote it up as a wound from enemy fire. No one questioned it. So now I'm two down and one to go."

What an upside-down world Briggs thought where people hoped to get wounded so they could get out of the shit and go home. He was sure Forhan thought he would get a million-dollar flesh wound, as opposed to be being blown to bits or dying from a sucking stomach wound.

"Hey, do you remember LaRoche?" Forhan asked.

"Yeah. Sure. Tom LaRoche. He was the guy at Pendleton that tried to get out of going to Vietnam by claiming he was a fag. Right?"

"Yep. One and the same. He's a fire team leader now in my squad. He's a bad ass. He's no fag. He's John Fucking Wayne. Up for a Bronze Star. He rescued a couple of dudes who were wounded during a fire fight. They were dead men if it hadn't been for LaRoche. I was a witness. Captain had me sign off on the citation."

"No shit? I don't get it. What was the fag story about?"

"When we were at Pendleton, he was having girlfriend problems. He figured the only way he could get out of going to Nam and keep the girl was by claiming he was a fruit. Of course, it didn't work."

"You sure he wasn't having boyfriend problems?"

"Nah. He's cool. I've seen pictures of the girlfriend. She's hot. But I think she found another guy and so LaRoche dedicated himself to killing gooks."

Briggs returned to full duty after two weeks and was sitting radio watch on Christmas morning. There had been talk of a holiday truce, but neither side trusted each other so nothing got past the rumor stage. During down time, the gun crews had painted "Merry Christmas Charlie" and "Happy New Year" on several shells. Routine fire missions continued to be called in.

"Ringo One this is Redwood six. Over."

"This is Ringo one, over."

"Fire mission. Two rounds, illumination at four, niner, six, six - five, eight, niner, six. Fire when ready."

"Roger Redwood." Briggs repeated the coordinates and passed on the information to the fire direction team. Barely more than a minute later the rounds were on their way.

"Redwood 6. This is Ringo 1. Rounds on the way."

"Roger Ringo."

Two minutes later Redwood 6 reported: "Mission complete. Thank you, Ringo." Briggs could visualize the yellowish illumination lighting up the terrain like Broadway on New Year's Eve. The flares wiggled as they descended at the end of strings attached to parachutes. The ground, buildings and trees also appeared to be wiggling.

It was rare that the enemy would be caught in the open. Even if they were moving around out there, they could hear the pop of the shells and would quickly take cover.

"Roger Redwood. Out." The radio returned to a low static that kept everyone in the bunker alert. With no other fire missions, they returned to reading books and writing letters.

Christmas seemed to Briggs to be occurring on a different planet. He had received the obligatory Christmas cards and letters from his family. Nothing from Brenda.

The American Red Cross distributed cards from anonymous strangers thanking them for their service. That was a bit of an empty gesture. It was hard to connect dots to the real world. The cooks again did their best to provide some resemblance of a holiday meal.

Briggs replayed in his mind his trip to Brenda's home, a year ago. He could see her family gathered around the fireplace in the den. Brenda would be dressed in a plaid skirt and a dark green sweater looking like a million bucks. Her smile always melted him. He missed her.

He could hear the cold rain continuing outside. It was zero four hundred hours on December 25 in Vietnam. That meant it was 4 p.m. the day before in Philadelphia. Her family would be getting ready to celebrate Christmas Eve. His family would be doing the same in Battle Creek where the riverfront park was decorated with thousands of twinkly lights.

It was easy to feel sorry for yourself at this time of year. He thought most everyone around him was feeling the same melancholy. There seemed to be a lot less conversation these days as men at war withdrew into themselves.

Briggs decided to write a letter to his family. His main goal was always to assure his mother that he was well and safe. He had not told his parents about the gunshot wound. That was news for when he was safely back stateside. He sent Christmas greetings and expressed how much he missed everyone.

He started to write a letter to Brenda. He had never felt as lonely as he did at this moment. He wanted to talk with her like they did when they were together. After a few starts and stops, he gave up. He had not heard from her since the summer. The relationship was over. He knew that any letter he wrote, he would want to get it back five minutes after putting it in the mail.

CHAPTER 28

January 1967
Firebase Chippewa - Indian Country
Thua Thien Province

Vietnam War Timeline: Operation Prairie One was winding down at a cost of 226 Marine KIA and over 1,700 enemy dead or captured. Operation Prairie 2 was launched February 1.

New Year's 1967 was celebrated by gun crew number three firing a random round at zero hundred hours into no man's land in Indian Country. It was a reckless act that could have fatal consequences for innocent civilians who happened to be in the wrong spot at the wrong time.

Their thinking, if it could be called that, was that nobody should be out walking around at midnight unless they were looking for trouble. They had fired at the same coordinates they had used an hour earlier on an H & I mission.

Guard post number five added to the celebration by firing their M-14s into the air. Posts two, six and seven shot off flares. The entire battery was scrambling for bunkers and fighting holes not knowing if it was party time or an enemy attack.

A newly arrived second lieutenant, Curtis Hornsby, was the duty officer in the FDC. This was Lieutenant Hornsby's second watch. He had been listening to radio traffic hoping for a quiet shift.

"What the fuck? What's going on?" Hornsby's first thought was that he had missed a scheduled H & I. A gun crew wasn't supposed to fire without his permission. Everyone in the FDC started to scramble.

"Tellish. Who the fuck is firing? What are they shooting at?" Tellish was manning the two landlines to the gun crews. He was already on the phones trying to find the guilty party.

"Sir. It was gun number three. They said Happy New Year."

"Happy New Year my ass," Hornsby responded.

The guard posts began to report in all claiming they had seen enemy movement around the perimeter.

There was speculation that Charlie or the NVA might have some New Year's presents for the Americans. Maybe this was it. But the firing stopped as quickly as it had started. The remainder of the night was quiet.

It appeared to have been a coordinated violation of the rules. Everyone expected that some serious penalty might be handed down. The brass huddled in the morning. The result was a Gunny Lincoln lecture at the next day's formation about unauthorized firing of weapons and the threat of serious consequences for any future incidents. Otherwise, all was forgiven as a harmless act of soldiers in war letting off steam.

"Briggs! The major wants to see your ass ASAP. Let's go. Move it." It was 0930 hours, on Wednesday, January 4, 1967. Eight months down, five to go. Briggs had just gotten off overnight radio watch. He was in his cot, fully clothed, with his partially full laundry sack pulled over his head to block out the daylight. He had made morning formation and then was trying to grab a couple hours of sleep before turning to supervising work parties and the never-ending preventive maintenance on the communications equipment. Plus, there was his daily meeting with Staff Sergeant Latham to review the watchlist for the next 48 hours.

The annoying self-important voice of recently promoted Lance Corporal Risdon cut through him like a chain saw. Risdon viewed himself as having the same command authority as the major.

"Sergeant!" Briggs shouted back in response without moving from his cot.

"What?"

"It's Sergeant Briggs to you Risdon, you fucking cunt."

"Well excuse me," Risdon responded in a mocking voice. "Sergeant Briggs. Please. Sir. Asshole. You are wanted by the CO."

Briggs sat up considering whether it was worth continuing the back and forth with Risdon. He decided not.

"I'll be there in a minute. Get out of here before I shoot you."

Briggs decided it was best not to keep the major waiting so once Risdon disappeared, he did a quick facewash using water from the five gallon can each hooch kept for drinking, washing, and shaving. He grabbed his web belt and M-14 and picked his way over to the CO's tent trying to avoid the standing puddles of water as much as possible.

As he approached the command hooch, he could see other bodies inside. He decided to do the military protocol thing knocking on the door and announcing: "Sir, Sergeant Briggs reporting as ordered. Request permission to enter."

"Enter."

Briggs felt it sounded too much like boot camp. As he stepped inside, he saw the XO and Gunny Lincoln both smiling. He figured they had found his entrance amusing. Major Cavalo was sitting at his field desk reading some papers.

"You wanted to see me sir?" That sounded more casual to Briggs' ears.

"Sergeant. We're sending one gun, its crew and an FO team up to Quang Tri to support the Ninth Marines. Operation Prairie. You drew the short straw. You and Lieutenant Hornsby are the FO team. I need an experienced NCO to be with him."

Briggs knew they were expecting him to state loud and clear, "Yes Sir," but he decided to remain mute as his silent challenge to military authority. It meant nothing to anyone but him. He was a bit surprised by this sudden change of events and wasn't sure how he felt about it, not that it mattered. Orders were orders.

Major Cavalo, tired of waiting for a response, finally looked up from his papers and said "Gunny Lincoln will give you further instructions. Not sure if we'll see you back here or not. Good luck."

"Thank you, Sir." Gunny Lincoln walked him out of the hooch.

"Sorry about that. I tried to keep you here, but there wasn't any other choice. I'm sure you and the LT will be a happy couple."

"It is what it is Gunny. Thanks for keeping me around here as long as you did. So now what? How do we get to Quang Tri?"

"Go grab your gear, say your goodbyes and meet over at the mess tent at thirteen hundred hours. Eat something first. You and Lieutenant Hornsby have a reservation on the next chopper out of here. The gun crew will follow."

"Which gun crew?"

"Lobo."

"He's your buddy, right?"

"You mean because he's a brother? You think all us black guys are supposed to love each other? That's not how it is. He knows what he's doing with that howitzer. He can hit a postage stamp from 10 miles. Personally? He's a slimeball. I don't trust him."

Staff Sergeant Milo M. Derby was 32 years old. He was an imposing figure. He stood 6'4" and weighed about 250 pounds. Besides lifting a lot of heavy ammunition during his 14 years in the Crotch, almost all of it served in the artillery, he had spent his spare time lifting weights in the gym. He always had an edge to him as if he were looking for a fight. Nobody messed with him.

He and his crew had nicknamed their howitzer "Lobo." The name was painted artfully in yellow on both sides of the howitzer barrel. Derby had adopted Lobo as his alter identity. No one called him Milo, or Derby, or Staff Sergeant. It was just "Lobo." A lobo is a timber wolf that lives in the southwestern United States. No one was sure why Derby had adopted the name.

Briggs had made it a point to steer clear of Lobo and the men in his crew who seemed to have taken on the same attitude as their leader.

Now they had no choice but to work together. They would be a team in Quang Tri.

The Marine Corps unofficial motto was "hurry up and wait." That meant if you were scheduled to leave at thirteen hundred, you might reasonably expect to leave at fourteen thirty. Not this time. Briggs looked at his watch as the helo lifted off from the LZ. It was 1306 hours. Firebase Chippewa had become home during the past few weeks. He did not expect to see it again.

"Good luck lad. Keep your head down and your powder dry," were the departing words from Gunny Lincoln. Briggs and Lincoln shook hands and hoped they would see each other again.

CHAPTER 29

January 1967
Second Battalion / Ninth Marines (2/9)
DMZ - Quang Tri Province

Vietnam War Timeline: Navy Commander James Stockdale, the senior U.S. prisoner of war, wrote out his first covert message with the list of the names of forty fellow American POWs in the Hanoi Hilton.

The men of Golf Company had been chasing the NVA for three months across the rice paddies, over and through mountain jungles and along the banks of the Ben Hai River which was the border between South and North Vietnam. This was the Demilitarized Zone, the DMZ, where there was supposed to be no combat.

They were constantly on the move. After days of patrolling, setting ambushes, multiple skirmishes with the NVA and 24-hour watches, they were worn out physically. Their equipment needed replacement. Three hours of sleep under a poncho in a fighting hole, day or night, was considered a luxury.

Rumors made the rounds that the entire battalion would be relieved at the conclusion of Operation Prairie and would be sent out of country for rest & relaxation. That was more wishful thinking than fact.

The company was now hunkered down behind barbed wire and sandbagged guard posts. Four large tents served as a mess hall, supply and temporary sleeping quarters for the few that weren't on duty.

Briggs and Hornsby were able to draw additional field (782) gear. Since they were operating as a team, they were expected to take care of each other in the field. They would work, fight, eat and sleep together. There was no upgrade available for officers. They were now attached at the hip.

It was the first time Briggs had worked closely with an officer that was younger than him. Briggs was older by almost a year. Calling him "sir" seemed awkward. Hornsby was trained as a helicopter pilot and was doing six months as a forward observer before he would return to the air wing.

Three days later Lobo and crew showed up. The big howitzer was the largest artillery available in that theater. It was considered "The King of Battle." Lobo was replacing another howitzer that had been towed away when its barrel wore out and simultaneously needed extensive engine work and a new track. It couldn't shoot and it couldn't move.

An additional 8" howitzer was expected to join them within the week. A battery of 105's from the 3rd Battalion, 12th Marines (3/12), and a couple of 155s had been the sole artillery support.

It took Lobo a half day to get dug in and operational. They created a separate, secure ammo dump. Though uninvited, Briggs and Hornsby decided it made the most sense that they would live with Lobo's crew.

There were no privates around that they could delegate to digging their fighting holes, so Briggs went ahead and began. Not knowing what to expect from the LT, he was happy when Hornsby joined in. The ground was still soft from the retreating monsoon season, so the digging was relatively easy. They would improve their living conditions the longer they were there. For now, they needed a hole in the ground in case of incoming.

Captain Leonard Palmore was the Echo Company Commander. Briggs had known him back at Lejeune when he was a Platoon Commander in Lima Company 3/8. Briggs remembered him as being a good guy, fair and respected by his men. He was also one of the few African American officers Briggs had known.

Hornsby, Briggs and Lobo were called to a meeting with Palmore to fill them in on an upcoming mission. S-2 (Intelligence) had reports that the NVA was re-infiltrating an area that the Marines had cleared the month before. Now they needed to go back. Nothing new about that. It was that kind of war. No one ever held any ground permanently.

"We're sending second platoon to check it out. Lieutenant Forrest will be in charge. Sergeant Haverhill is second in command. We want to get the FO team in place. Once you guys can confirm the bad guys are there, I want you to blow the shit out of them," Palmore said.

Both Hornsby and Lobo responded: "yes sir." Briggs nodded in agreement.

"You'll be leaving tonight at 2100 hours. You got some humping to do to be in position by daylight. Your call sign is Whitehorse two-six. Go check in with Lieutenant Forrest. He'll get you set up with ammo and rations and fill you in on your walk in the woods.

"Staff Sergeant Derby, or Lobo, or whatever you call yourself, go check in with the FDC and make sure you're all on the same page. Good luck men."

Hornsby and Briggs found second platoon gathered around their fighting holes. Several men were warming up C rations over fuel tablets. Forrest was sitting in a bunker cleaning his sawed-off shotgun. He was short and stocky. Muscular arms stuck out from his shirt sleeves. He had blond hair and blue eyes. A red scar ran across the bottom of his jaw line.

"We have about three miles to hump tonight. We should be in position by midnight. We'll set up a perimeter and hang on until daylight. Then we'll hump a couple more miles. We've been on this route before. We know it. So does the NVA. They know we know it. It's the game we play with each other. They might set up some ambushes, so we'll need to take a couple diversions.

"I want you men to stick close to Sergeant Haverhill. Do what he tells you to do. He's out checking on the men getting them ready for the mission. He'll be back here in a few minutes.

"If we find what they tell us that we'll find, a battalion of NVA, we will get you in position to call in your guns and blow the shit out of them. I don't need any rookie mistakes out there. Your only job on this mission is to get that artillery fire on target. Got it?"

Hornsby and Briggs responded simultaneously, "Yes sir."

Haverhill was the opposite of Forrest. He was tall, raw boned and spoke with the deep, gravelly Cajun baritone accent of his Louisiana upbringing. He carried an M-14 and a .45 caliber pistol.

Neither Forrest nor Haverhill were particularly warm and fuzzy. They were all business. They had done this before. FOs had come and gone. Some were better than others. One past FO was known as "Lieutenant Short Round," an obvious dig at his inability to put rounds on target.

Briggs figured that he and Hornsby stuck out as being as green as they were. They would have to prove themselves in the field. They were the new men on the hill.

Haverhill gave them an extra look over checking their gear, ammo and weapons making sure that there were no loose parts that would rattle as they moved. He helped them strip down some C-ration packets that would have to make do for the three days they were expected to be out before extraction or resupply.

Both Hornsby and Briggs were carrying M-14s, with four magazines. They noticed that the grunts carried twice as much ammo. Briggs had the PRC-25 Radio and two extra batteries. Hornsby had two additional batteries in his pack and a map case. They each had four canteens, helmets, flak jackets and an entrenching tool.

A full platoon would have forty-one men plus attachments such as corpsmen, snipers and the FOs. It could total as many as 50. It was rare that a platoon had its full component. This one was no exception. Haverhill had called everyone into formation. Briggs did a quick count in the dark and came up with 26.

Forrest and Haverhill communicated in hushed tones as they directed the platoon out of the compound. No one else spoke. They all knew the drill. Hornsby and Briggs followed.

Second squad was assigned the point. The middle of the formation consisted of the first squad, Forrest, Haverhill, their radio operator and corpsman. Hornsby and Briggs were with the third squad that covered their rear. Forrest wanted Briggs to be separated from the other radio operator by an adequate distance.

At first, they split into two columns on either side of a well-worn path. This was friendly territory. Briggs was surprised at how quiet 26 men could be walking with full equipment in a combat zone at night. There was no rattling of loose equipment. No talking.

After about a mile the pace slowed, and the column switched to single file. Now they were spread out more than 60 yards from front to back, each man maintaining about three yards distance from each other. The only noise Briggs heard was an occasional trip or stumble. It was inevitable with this many men walking in the dark. He concentrated on every footstep to make sure he was not one of them.

It was shortly after midnight that the column was halted, a perimeter formed, and listening posts set out. Briggs checked in with the FDC, whispering into his handset the way he had heard so many do when he was on the other end.

"Rabbit Three this is Whitehorse two six. Radio check. Over."

"Roger Whitehorse. I hear you loud and clear. Over." It gave Briggs a warm feeling that there was someone on the other end. He reported their coordinates which Hornsby had confirmed. This was home until daylight.

CHAPTER 30

February 1967
Second Platoon - Golf Company – 2/9
DMZ - Quang Tri Province

Vietnam War Timeline: Two major search and destroy missions against the VC were launched in the Mekong Delta and the Iron Triangle by combined U.S. Army, Marine and ARVN units. Operation Deckhouse Five and Cedar Falls were considered unproductive. It was believed that the VC had been forewarned of the attacks. Seventy-nine Americans were killed.

A red tinge began to break over the horizon about zero four thirty hours. The word was passed that they would move out in ten minutes. It was more ready time than necessary. No one had slept. This was routine work for the grunts. This was only day one of what was supposed to be a three-day patrol. They all knew from experience that it could turn into a ten-day patrol.

Hornsby and Briggs felt they were moving like an anchor. They were soft from doing their work in the relative comfort of an FDC bunker. It was going to be a difficult day of keeping up.

The first night had been spent in a hilly, forested area that reminded Briggs of Michigan. By 0600 the sun was up, and the platoon was working its way along the edge of a wide stretch of devastation created by American defoliant spraying of the mangrove forests less than two weeks before.

The goal was to destroy the crops that provided food supply for the enemy, deprive them of cover and flush them into the open where the Americans had the advantage of firepower. Dead trees, plants and animals had turned the forest and adjoining agricultural land into a moonscape.

The temperature and the humidity had risen steadily as the sun appeared on a rare, almost cloudless day. Briggs was drenched in sweat. He had four canteens but even observing strict water discipline he knew that wouldn't last him. When the patrol stopped at zero eight hundred hours for food and a rest break, he was gassed. Hornsby wasn't doing any better.

"Sergeant. Do you want me to take the radio? Give you a break?" Hornsby asked.

He didn't have to ask twice. Briggs turned the 20-pound PRC-25 over to him without a word and shot the LT a thankful grin. Briggs had wondered if they were going to be a team, or whether he was going to be Hornsby's lackey. The lieutenant was showing himself to be a team player.

The rest of the morning was stop and go, as the point moved cautiously checking out possible ambush sites, booby traps and what appeared to have been an NVA camp site.

At each stop Hornsby pulled out his map case and updated their coordinates which Briggs relayed over the radio in whispered tones to the FDC. It was crucial that artillery always knew where the friendlies were located.

As darkness descended the word was passed that they would dig in for the night. Sergeant Haverhill set up the perimeter and listening posts. Team Hornsby was assigned a position in the middle of the perimeter, separated from the other radio operator by enough distance to eliminate the chance that they both could be wiped out by a single explosive round.

Briggs was impressed as he watched Haverhill plan the night's defenses. He was the ultimate NCO, a "lean and mean, green killing machine." Nobody questioned his knowledge or his authority. Briggs was glad they were on the same team. Haverhill was like having a warm blanket, a sense of security.

Team Hornsby dug out a small impression and spread their ponchos. It wasn't textbook but it would give them some protection from incoming fire. Briggs was assigned a perimeter position at zero two hundred hours. Hornsby would be left by himself on radio watch.

As they settled down with their C-rations Briggs took inventory of himself. He was sore all over from hiking the uneven ground and constant shifting of his equipment. The straps from the pack and the radio had dug into his shoulders. He also was dealing with a headache and a couple rashes that popped up on his left arm and neck. There was no ready cure. The corpsman gave him aspirin and lubricating ointment, but it didn't do any good. He would just have to deal with it.

The night proceeded without incident. Briggs felt fortunate that he had caught two hours of uncomfortable sleep waking every time he shifted position. The headache had come and gone.

Day two was more of the same except that the clouds returned providing some relief from the heat. Just a lot of trudging over hills, through woods, crossing streams. They passed through more areas of defoliation where puffs of mist were kicked up by their boots.

Conversation was minimal. During one break, Hornsby observed "we might not shoot a lot of gooks, but we seem to be doing a great job of killing off all the plants and animals in this country."

At one of the stream crossings, most everyone re-filled their canteens popping in their water purification tablets. Water was water. It was necessary regardless of how bad the taste and how it looked.

Day two finished like day one. Just an excruciating hike, finding little evidence of NVA activity. Briggs watched Haverhill build the perimeter using the natural landscape to the platoon's advantage. He knew exactly how to create overlapping fields of fire, where to position the automatic weapons and even created a small reserve force in case of a breakthrough. If he hadn't written the textbook on how to set up the defense, he certainly had read it.

After Team Hornsby was settled in Briggs said, "Hey LT. I was just thinking about our job out here. We need to be ready to pull the trigger when Forrest gives us the word. Neither one of us has ever done this before from this end. Maybe we should call in a mission or two, adjust the fire and see if we know what we're doing."

"You mean just pick a random target and call it in?"

"No different than the nightly H & I mission, only we would be providing new coordinates. There's nothing out there, except prairie dogs, snakes and swamp rats. If we happen to hit an NVA sneaking around by mistake, well, that's a bonus."

Hornsby thought about it for a couple minutes. "I would need to get permission from Lieutenant Forrest."

"I can assure you that Staff Sergeant Lobo is sitting back there at firebase shit hole with his itchy finger on the trigger of that howitzer, waiting for the chance to blow the crap out of something," Briggs argued.

"Well, let me go check and see what the lieutenant says. It's his call."

Briggs was feeling that he and Hornsby had connected. They had overcome the "officer – enlisted" thing. Briggs had three more years of experience in the crotch, which Hornsby respected. They were relying on each other. They had become partners.

Twenty minutes later Hornsby returned. "We got the go ahead. Suspected NVA concentration. Coordinates four eight niner six, three two seven seven. One round of illumination, a marking round and three rounds of H-E."

"Roger that Mr. Hornsby. Time to fire up Lobo and fuck with the bad boys."

Briggs took a few deep breaths, pressed the call button on the handset: "Rabbit Three this is Whitehorse two six. Fire Mission." In his mind's eye he could see scrambling going on in the FDC where everyone was probably in a rest position smoking cigarettes and drinking coffee.

"Roger Whitehorse. Ready to copy."

Briggs repeated the coordinates Hornsby had given him and ordered the one round of illumination. He felt a slight bit of guilt when he said "suspected NVA position."

Rabbit Three read back the coordinates and the one round of illumination.

"Roger. Fire when ready," Briggs said. It was the first time he had ever requested a round to be fired. He had always been the middleman before.

There was silence from the other end for about twenty seconds before Briggs heard "On the way."

They could hear the shell pass overhead and suddenly exploded about 500 feet above the ground turning the landscape into an eerie sort of daylight. They watched as the giant flare floated down. The target they had chosen was about a mile away.

"Same coordinates. One round of H-E. Will adjust fire," Hornsby said.

Briggs repeated that into the radio. Within a minute the marking round was on its way, this one exploding in a fiery blast of gunpowder, shrapnel and dirt. It took a few seconds for the sound to reach them.

"Drop 50. Right 100. Three rounds of H-E. Fire for Effect," Hornsby said. He was looking through binoculars although Briggs was sure he could see adequately without them. The flare was still lighting the landscape.

Briggs repeated the instructions. Within a minute the rounds were on their way. Even though they were just blowing up dirt, there was a feeling of exhilaration.

After the last round was fired, Briggs said, "Cease fire. End of mission."

"Roger Whitehorse. Cease fire," the Rabbit Three operator said. "After mission report requested."

They were expected to provide some body count or vehicles destroyed. Hornsby would have to falsify the results. That was an offense that could be prosecuted, but rarely happened. How would anyone be able to prove it?

Hornsby said: "Tell them troops were in the open. Possible 3 KIA." Briggs relayed the report making him a co-conspirator. Team Hornsby shook hands. They were no longer virgins.

CHAPTER 31

February 8, 1967
Second Platoon – Golf Company (2/9)
DMZ - Quang Tri Province

Vietnam Timeline: U.S. President Lyndon Johnson sent a letter to Ho Chi Minh, by way of Moscow, that began "Dear Mr. President: I am writing to you in the hope that the conflict in Viet Nam can be brought to an end," and outlining his proposal that "I am prepared to order a cessation of bombing against your country... as soon as I am assured that infiltration into South Viet Nam by land and by sea has stopped." Fifteen Americans were killed that day. Their names are on Panel 15E -Lines 8, 9 and 10 of "The Wall."

To no one's surprise the three-day patrol was extended. There was a helo drop of food and water on day four. There was no need for any additional ammo since no one had fired a weapon. Two grunts were airlifted out. One suffering from extreme bouts of diarrhea, nausea and a rash that seemingly had consumed his entire body. The other had a broken ankle when he tripped over tree roots and stepped into a deep hole. Everyone heard the crack of his bone. He screamed in pain. Unable to walk, he was holding up the rest of the platoon. He was carried to the LZ.

There were other cases of illness but not enough to get a ride out.

Everyone had the rash. The corpsman said it was jungle itch. The lubricating ointment continued to be worthless.

Day six passed into day seven. There still was no enemy sighting. Just more humping up and down the hills, through mangrove forests, crossing streams, skirting the edges of rice paddies. Forrest and Haverhill were cautious and deliberate. There were no hasty decisions.

They huddled several times each day over their maps. As second in command by virtue of his rank, Hornsby was included in the strategy meetings. He mostly kept his mouth shut. He was a passenger not a conductor. Haverhill was the real boss.

A few times the point halted the platoon as they investigated what appeared to be enemy campsites. They checked for booby traps and ambushes. Forrest marked every place they investigated on his map.

It seemed to be an endless search. The monsoon season had waned, but that didn't mean the rain had stopped entirely. Long ago they had given up on trying to be comfortable. Rain, sun, mud, dust, heat, humidity, bugs, weed killer. It all contributed to their overall misery.

Despite their exhaustion, no one seemed to lose concentration. They were constantly on the alert. The resupply had been necessary for them to stay in the field longer, but each chopper visit announced to the NVA their location. Briggs had a feeling that they were being watched from the dark green hills that dotted the landscape. He was sure that the hunters had become the hunted.

When the platoon stopped, Briggs was struck with how quiet the surrounding area became. No war noises. No people noise. No animal noises.

"It's quiet out there," Briggs whispered to Hornsby.

"Too quiet," the LT responded. They shared a laugh about the bad western movie cliché they had just repeated.

After a few days of poking around enemy territory, there was a feeling that soldiers knew when their time was coming. They talked about it among themselves even though it wasn't necessary. It was a shared communication born of experience.

As daylight began to fade, they entered a shallow valley where they would spend the night. Haverhill immediately began to set up his defenses.

Hill 109 was off to their left. It was one of the smaller hills in the area. Forrest pointed to the top where he wanted Hornsby and Briggs to establish their OP. He sent two men with them to provide protection and to be another listening post.

The climb was harder than it looked up a wet slope covered with tangled roots and rocks. About 70 feet shy of the summit they found a dry creek bed that provided a shallow gulley for protection. Briggs thought Haverhill would be proud of them using the natural landscape to their advantage.

Hornsby felt it provided a good enough vantage point. If the NVA began throwing mortar shells up there they would aim for the top of the hill. The shrapnel would fly over their heads.

They dug in for the night. The two grunts each took a position looking outward with the artillerymen and their radio between them. Even though the gully gave them some protection you can never be deep enough when the shooting starts. Using their entrenching tools, they each scraped out their own hole in the rocky soil.

Briggs called their coordinates into the FDC. He usually found comfort in hearing a familiar voice on the other end. But since he had not been in the unit long before being sent on the patrol, he didn't recognize who he was now talking to.

In the fading daylight Hornsby got busy scribbling landmarks on his map. He noted what looked like four potential targets that could be possible enemy cover or paths of attack. His visibility was about three miles before the landscape faded behind hills and trees. There was also a small barnlike structure next to a dyke. A path led from there and disappeared into a stand of trees two hundred yards beyond.

Briggs relayed the coordinates of the targets to the FDC giving each one a fire mission number that would save time in case they needed support in a hurry. They also marked targets within a hundred yards of their own perimeter. This would be their last line of defense in case they were attacked.

Briggs and Hornsby cleaned their weapons and magazines. Learning how to take apart and put together a M-14 and a .45 caliber pistol in the dark was part of their training.

They shared some cheese with crackers and one can of lima beans with ham. It was all that was left from the resupply three days before. They would worry about tomorrow when tomorrow came. Relief had to come soon.

Radio checks were conducted every fifteen minutes both with the FDC and bottom of the hill. No one was expected to sleep.

Haverhill had three listening posts each out 50 yards. The posts all had a PRC-6. Hornsby also had a PRC-6 so he could talk directly to Forrest.

A light drizzle began shortly after midnight. The clouds blocked the moonlight. It was dark as dark could be. That's when the first observation post got probed. The NVA were not sure where the Marines were, so they had thrown a grenade hoping to draw fire and expose their location.

The Marines on the OP held their fire. They started to crawl towards the perimeter whispering into the radio "post two on the way home route number one." They had pre-numbered two different escape routes earlier so that they wouldn't get shot by friendly fire.

Hornsby whispered into his radio asking Forrest if he wanted artillery illumination. Forrest told him to hold off. He didn't want to show his hand yet.

Briggs clicked his handset to call Rabbit Three and whispered: "Enemy activity. Wait five."

"Roger Whitehorse. Wait five. Good luck."

Nothing happened for twenty minutes. Dead silence. "It was quiet. Too quiet," Briggs thought. It was his own private joke.

Then an automatic weapon opened fire on the right flank. It was answered immediately. Suddenly there was shooting from all directions. Two claymore mines exploded. Briggs could hear human screams.

He felt like he was watching a movie from the balcony as the battle below quickly reached full fury. Grenades exploded. Small arms fire was constant. Green tracer bullets spit from the machine guns. Two enemy mortar rounds exploded just outside the Marine perimeter.

The two grunts on the hill with the FO team weren't sure what they should do. From their place on the hill, they could shoot down and help the Marines below but were fearful of shooting the wrong people in the dark and didn't want to give away their position. Two hand flares had been fired but were insufficient to provide much view of the landscape. They needed the additional candlepower provided by the artillery rounds.

"Briggs. I just got the word from Forrest. Call for illumination," Hornsby ordered.

"Yes sir."

"Rabbit this is Whitehorse. Fire mission one. Two rounds Illumination."

"Roger Whitehorse. Two rounds daylight."

Fifteen seconds later Briggs heard: "On the way." As the shooting below increased it seemed to take forever for the giant flares to arrive on scene, explode and light up the battlefield. When they did it looked like a night game at Yankee Stadium.

"Shit. There's a gazillion fucking rats down there," Hornsby shouted. Some of the NVA soldiers hit the ground trying to avoid being seen, but most of them kept moving forward firing their weapons. The Marines were mowing them down.

Hornsby quickly reviewed his list of pre-set fire missions knowing that it was time to walk some of the big guns into the fight.

"Fire mission number three, two rounds H E," he shouted to Briggs, who repeated it into the radio. "Tell them we will adjust."

Now that they could see with the light of the flare, the two grunts with the FO team opened fire.

"Roger Whitehorse. On the way."

They could hear the big shells pass overhead. Briggs felt the sound was like sitting under an expressway viaduct as trucks roared past. They saw the flash of the fireball before they heard the explosions and the ground shook. The big guns could change the face of the battle quickly.

"Drop 25. Fire for effect," Hornsby ordered. No left or right adjustments were necessary. He wanted to walk the shells in closer to the Marine lines where he could see the battle raging. Briggs noticed that Hornsby's voice had risen a few octaves with the excitement of the moment. He relayed the LT's instructions.

"Roger Whitehorse. Repeat. Fire for effect."

The grunts with Team Hornsby had given away their position once they started shooting. Now small arms fire from below had begun to find them. The mortar rounds were sure to follow. The NVA would want to take out the FO team that was calling in the artillery.

Hornsby yelled at the two Marines who were still in their position to cease fire. "Go down below if you want to start shooting at them," he shouted. They didn't need to be told twice.

He immediately regretted letting them both go. They were now alone on the hill. Their focus was on directing the artillery fire. They would be toast if the NVA attacked their position. A couple of mortar rounds had landed near the top of the hill just close enough to remind them to keep their heads down.

Hornsby kept directing fire left and right of what he had marked as his meridian line from a point 500 yards in front of the Marine positions down to 100 yards. That was the absolute closest he would want to get. Illumination rounds continued to turn night into day.

Briggs could feel his adrenaline pumping. He and Hornsby were a smooth functioning team as the huge rounds found their targets and began turning the tide. This was the way artillery and infantry were supposed to work.

There were six points of communication to launching a successful artillery attack. Hornsby and Briggs, the FOs, were point one and two. The FDC radio operator was number three. He relayed the information to the FDC, a lieutenant assisted by an NCO, who calculated the direction and trajectory of the guns. They double checked each other's reckoning. That was point number 4. When they agreed on the numbers, it was relayed by wire or radio to the gun crew, point number 5.

The gun crew chief, Staff Sergeant Lobo, oversaw his team getting the correct adjustment on the gun and right powder amounts before pulling the lanyard. That was point number 6.

Mistakes can occur at any point. It is not unlike the party game known as "Pass A Secret," in which a person whispers a message to the next person and the story is passed on to several others with inaccuracies accumulating as the game proceeds.

An FO under extreme pressure, working in the dark, could read his map wrong and provide faulty coordinates. Radio communication isn't guaranteed to be clear during battle. A radio operator may say or hear the wrong words and pass it on to the FDC where calculations are made using incorrect data. Or a mistake could be made by a gun crew working fast to get rounds on their way.

The after-battle report never was able to determine why one round landed short, just above where the FOs were conducting their business. Briggs was relaying coordinates for a new target when his radio went silent. His last words to Rabbit Three were: "...fire for effect."

Once Lieutenant Forrest realized that his FO team had been knocked out he called for air support. A U.S. Air Force C-47 nicknamed "Puff the Magic Dragon," had been circling a few miles south of the DMZ waiting for a call.

The Marines marked their lines with blue smoke. Outside that line was fair game. Anyone who ever witnessed the frightening firepower unleashed by "Puff" never forgot the sight or the sound of the multiple mounted machine guns pouring out lead like an old time Gatling Gun.

The steady line of tracer bullets looked as if one could use it as a walkway to the airplane. The sound resembled a jet engine on takeoff. No one survived at the bottom of its river of bullets.

One ground to air rocket was fired by the NVA but missed. It took "Puff" two flybys to silence the battlefield. Then "Puff" moved quickly out of the area but told ground control they would be available if they were needed again.

Lieutenant Forrest's radio operator connected with the FDC and explained the silence from the FO team. A detail was sent up the hill to investigate.

Just before the short round exploded Hornsby had stood up to get a better view of the battlefield. It was a rookie mistake. He was cut in half. All that was found of him was his legs and feet still wearing his boots.

Briggs had stayed low. Most of the shrapnel sprayed overhead. His left side, which had faced uphill, took most of the damage. His arm was torn and hanging from the shoulder socket. He was bleeding from multiple wounds. His eardrums were shattered. One piece of hot metal had pierced his helmet and was sticking out of his head.

The corpsman who gave him triage wasn't sure if he was alive. Briggs was on the second Med Evac chopper out. There were others ahead of him with a better chance of being saved.

The rest of the patrol was helo lifted out later that day. There were nine Marine KIA, the first casualties of Operation Prairie Two.

PART III

"All gave some, some gave all."
Korean War Purple Heart Recipient
Sargent Howard W. Osterkamp, U.S. Army
Later Popularized by a Billy Ray Cyrus song - 1992

CHAPTER 32

April 1966
Fredericksburg, Virginia

A month had passed since Briggs left for Camp Pendleton. He was now headed overseas.

He wrote Brenda two letters hoping after each one that she would write him back. He apologized for not talking over his decision with her in advance. He hoped this would not be the end of their relationship. He stuck to the line that it was something he felt he had to do. He was a Marine.

Brenda never felt worse in her life. After she left the hotel room she had gone back to her dorm. She was not the type that cried easily but she couldn't hold back the tears this time. Since her roommate Mary Thorsen had gone home for the weekend Brenda had the room to herself. She was sure she would be able to get a handle on everything by the time Mary returned.

She was mad. She was hurt. She was sad. She was bitter. That week she tried her best to keep it to herself and act normal around her friends. She didn't do a particularly good job of it though as Mary asked her several times what was wrong.

Boyfriend problems were always the best guess. Brenda usually would tell Mary about her dates with Briggs, what they had done and what they were going to do. This time she was a blank screen.

After Briggs' second letter, Brenda decided she had to talk about it. Mary was a ready listener.

"He just up and decided like that to go to Vietnam? Nobody made him do it? Why would he do that? Why would anyone do that," Mary asked.

"I have no answer. He just said this is what he was meant to do. He's a Marine. It was his turn to go. They think different than we do. All of them. I met his friends at Camp Lejeune. They all think the same way. It's some macho male crap."

"What are you supposed to do while he's off playing with his guns?"

"I don't know. I never thought of myself as being a war bride waiting for my man to come home."

"You aren't pregnant, are you?" Mary asked.

"No. Of course not. Why would you say something like that?"

"I don't know. I thought maybe you told him you were pregnant, and he decided that it was time to get out of Dodge City. It's happened before. That's why our mothers tell us to stay away from sailors," Mary said flashing a smile.

Brenda did not respond. She was now dealing with tears. She flashed Mary an angry glance.

"Sorry. I was just trying to lighten the mood here a bit."

"Don't joke about this. It's not funny. What if he dies over there? His last thoughts of me would be 'what a bitch.' I can't live with that. I've actually thought that maybe if I had been pregnant, he wouldn't have gone."

"Are you going to write him back? You need to do that. You can't just ignore him."

"I might see this differently if the Marine Corps had made the decision to send him. Then he would have to go. He would have no choice. But, he decided on his own that he would go. Do you know how that makes me feel? I feel abandoned. I feel that our relationship meant nothing to him. I'll see you in a year honey."

They both fell silent.

"You'll find a new boyfriend."

"Mary," Brenda said raising her voice with a tone of indignation. "This isn't about finding a new boyfriend. I don't want a new boyfriend. I want my old boyfriend. I'm really pissed at him. This hurts.

"I understand that we only knew each other for six months. There were no commitments, but we were making plans for when he got out and I graduated. He and the Marine Corps had known each other for three years before he met me. I guess I was the loser in that competition."

"What did your parents think of him? They liked him, didn't they?"

"My mother doesn't like anyone. When he came home with me she just acted like he was part of the furniture. She even got drunk the night we all went to the country club for dinner. She didn't say much to him or about him. I'm used to that. I can live with it. That's just how she is."

"What about your father?"

"I think he liked him. I know that he admired him. He thought it was cool that Johnny was a Marine. Dad was never in the military and always felt he should have served. That's how that generation thinks about those things. He even asks about Johnny when we talk."

Brenda and Mary talked for two hours. It allowed Brenda to unload. That helped. She didn't feel quite as angry as she had. She went home on spring break a week later. Being home reminded her of his visit over the holidays. She couldn't help but miss him. She kept family conversation to a minimum telling her parents she was recovering from a bout with the flu. They left her alone.

Her mother, as Brenda expected, never asked about Briggs. She told her father that he was overseas but left out the details. "He drew the short straw. They're sending lots of people over there." Her father never asked for more information. He wasn't the type to dig into his daughter's private life.

Brenda had her good and bad days. She couldn't get rid of the feeling that he had gone to get away from her. She experienced an overwhelming sense of loss. Eventually, she decided to write Briggs a letter. There could be no closure without some sort of response to him.

She kept it short and non-committal. She avoided discussion of their split and anything specific he had said in his letters. She stuck to safe topics like school, family and friends. She figured the less said about their relationship, the better.

They had exchanged photographs some time ago. She couldn't throw his away, but she didn't want to be carrying it around with her either. He had given her both his high school and Marine Corps Boot Camp graduation photos. There were also four photos of them together including one with her family at Christmas. They all went into an envelope with other memorabilia.

She had seen the news clips of soldiers in Vietnam with photos of their girlfriends snapped inside a black rubber band around their helmet. It made her sick to think of her torn and tattered photo being carried in the jungle of Southeast Asia. She had this image of him having been shot and dying, his last moments on Earth clutching her picture. She knew that was Hollywood movie stuff, but it was difficult to get it out of her mind.

Graduation was looming a month away. Her parents and brother were making plans to come to Fredericksburg for the ceremony and then pack up her things and return to Ardmore. They wanted to celebrate with dinner at Fredericksburg's finest restaurant. Thinking about it deepened her sadness at the thought that Briggs would not be there. Since they had been together, she had often thought about graduation day. They had talked about him being there with her family. Now all she could do was to fight off a feeling of emptiness.

She wondered if Briggs would be thinking about her on that day. Would he remember? It was impossible for her to imagine what his life was like.

Brenda was sure that during her last semester of school she would find her first real job, perhaps in a different exciting city. Recruiters often visited campus. The college career services office provided leads and job search tips. Professors offered advice and networking ideas. Her friends exchanged thoughts on their plans. Brenda had always been a part of those discussions.

But once Briggs left, a spark went out. She had to deal with his absence and a feeling that she had been dumped for another mistress, the Marine Corps. She missed him and worried about him constantly. She floated through the final three months of school without applying for any jobs or making plans.

Bart Kiley got Brenda a job for the summer at his law firm as an assistant to an assistant. He was hoping she would catch the fever and go to law school. Living at home and working in her father's office, had not been her number one plan upon graduation.

CHAPTER 33

Monday, February 11, 1991
Fair Lawn, New Jersey

The kids were off to school. Jay had left early for the office. Brenda had the house to herself before her Monday afternoon tennis game. She had made the beds and done a quick clean up after a busy weekend of family visits and a Sunday afternoon birthday party for her youngest son Steven who had turned fourteen.

She sat with a cup of coffee and leisurely read the New York Times. She hadn't had time the day before to finish the Sunday papers. Now she was playing catch up.

With so much to read, she flew through the pages glancing at headlines that caught her attention. Her first time through she passed by the headline:

"On Memorial to the Dead, 14 Who Live."

She went on to scan the business section, sports, arts and entertainment. The revival of "Fiddler on the Roof" was playing to strong audiences at the Gershwin. The Broadway opening of "Miss Saigon" was scheduled for April.

The price of a U.S. Postage stamp was increased from 25 cents to 29 cents. Lithuania voted for independence from the U.S.S.R. The Knicks lost again and so did the Rangers. Baseball spring training camps would open in two weeks.

On her final flip through the front section to see if she missed anything important, Brenda read the first sentence of the Associated Press story she had previously overlooked.

> *Fourteen Americans can visit the Vietnam Veterans Memorial and find their names carved in black granite among the names of those killed in the war.*
>
> *"It was kind of scary," said Eugene Lauer, who lost part of both legs in Vietnam. "It's like seeing your name on a gravestone."*
>
> *Mr. Lauer's name is there because he was mistakenly listed as dead when a Government clerk typed a wrong number into a computer. All 14 records have been corrected, but the names in the continual chronological list on the memorial cannot easily be erased from the polished granite.*

Brenda took a deep breath as thoughts of Johnny Briggs flashed through her mind. She had thought of him often in the past three years since she had found his name on The Wall. She had wanted to find out how he had died and where he was buried.

She was intimidated by the effort she thought it would take and considered it a project for the future when she had more time in her life. How their relationship ended so many years ago still nagged at her like an annoying paper cut.

> *Mr. Lauer's journey to The Wall began on an October morning in 1970 as a sergeant with the 3rd Marine Division when he tripped a land mine on a reconnaissance patrol in the mountainous jungle west of Hue.*
>
> *Twenty years later, Mr. Lauer, 41 years old, sought treatment for post-traumatic stress syndrome and "part of the treatment was that I went down to The Wall," which is not far from his home in West Virginia.*

Standing under a nearly full moon on a mild night last April, he flipped through the paperback directory of names on the wall, looking for friends. He turned to the L's in a search for a cousin who had died in the war.

He not only found his cousin's name, but he also found his own name.

A Department of Defense spokesperson explained that the mistakes were due to clerical errors and that there was now an ongoing effort to correct the records.

The DOD was working with the Vietnam Veterans Memorial Fund (VVMF), the non-profit organization that was the primary force in getting The Wall built, to ensure accuracy on the Memorial.

The only way a name could be removed from The Wall is if a panel cracked and was replaced. A National Park Service supervisor said the fund (VVMF) had bought blank granite and errors could be removed if a panel was replaced.

The article listed the names of those who had not yet been found, then concluded with one final interview.

Former marine, John F. Briggs, 47, of Battle Creek, Michigan, heard about his name being included from a relative who had read an article published by The Detroit Free Press listing those from Michigan killed in the war.

Briggs is a well-known advocate on behalf of Agent Orange victims. He was in Washington, DC attending a Veterans' Affairs meeting when he was contacted for this article.

"I was surprised that I didn't hear about it sooner," Briggs said. "I guess that people who know me and have been to The Wall, never bothered to look for my name or they thought it was a different John Briggs. Since I'm alive I certainly never thought to look for myself."

Borrowing a line from Mark Twain, Briggs commented:
"The rumors of my death have been greatly exaggerated."
Briggs' name is on Panel 15E with his comrades who died
during Operation Prairie 2 in early February 1967.

Reviewing her thoughts later Brenda figured that she must have sat without moving and barely breathing for at least five minutes. She knew that tears had streaked her face. She read the story over several times.

What she wanted to know now was what had happened to him and why? What was his life like now? Had he thought of her like she had thought of him? Was he married? Did he have children? What was his job?

She thought of their family trip two years before when they had spent a week with Jay's Midwest relatives at a cottage on Lake Michigan. They had driven across Michigan on I-94 passing the Battle Creek exits. The idea of him being alive and still living there was not possible. Now she realized it could have been.

How would she have reacted if they had coincidentally bumped into each other? Michigan is a big place, but these things do happen. Fate does cross paths.

She wanted to talk with someone. She needed to share this news. Brenda and Jay had told each other about their prior relationships but details were slim. That was best for their marriage. She wasn't comfortable discussing this with him now.

Mary Thorsen was the only other person who knew the depth of their relationship. She had provided friendship when Brenda needed it most.

But Mary and Brenda had drifted apart staying in touch only with Christmas cards and empty promises of "let's find a time to get together." Mary now lived in California with husband number three, who Brenda had never met. Brenda had Mary's phone number but felt that a call would be awkward.

This was news she was going to have to keep to herself, at least for now. This was more than just hearing news about an old friend.

She remained distracted through the rest of her day. Being one of the better players at her tennis club her friends were surprised when she lost both her matches to players she had always easily beaten.

Steven's Junior Varsity basketball team had a game after school. Brenda looked forward to watching her boys play sports and socializing with the other parents. This game she decided to sit apart wanting time to deal with her own thoughts.

Fortunately, there was no need that night for a family dinner which would require chit chat and sharing what each person had done that day.

Steven would be tired from basketball and be satisfied with a quick meal of Mac and Cheese. Her older son, Eric, a trombone player in the school orchestra, had a rehearsal for the spring musical performance. Jay had a client dinner meeting and was taking a late train home from Manhattan. She didn't expect to see him until after 10 p.m.

Brenda dealt with mixed thoughts all day. She knew she should feel elated that a friend, particularly this friend, had survived the war. Yet, she felt guilty because she still harbored sadness about how their relationship ended. She wanted the closure that she had never gotten.

CHAPTER 34

March 1991
Fair Lawn, New Jersey

Two weeks passed since Brenda had read about the mistakes on The Wall. She watched the news for further updates and went to the public library to see if she could find other information. So far, she had turned up nothing additional.

She thought about calling the Vietnam Veterans Memorial Fund but couldn't push herself to that point. Briggs had been a boyfriend not family. She didn't feel that she had a right to ask them for information when there were at least 14 families who would be first in line. They deserved more attention than she did.

One day she picked up the phone to call Directory Assistance, thinking that she would ask for a number listed for John Briggs in Battle Creek, Michigan. Even if there was a listing for him, she didn't think she had the nerve to call him. She hung up the phone before dialing 411.

Brenda and her friend, Debbie Shaw, had started a marketing firm together four years before. They worked out of their homes meeting with clients at their offices or in coffee shops. The business was called: "Big Ideas Marketing." Their clients were local small businesses such as charities, specialty retail stores, lawyers and accountants that needed help with their advertising and marketing.

They weren't getting rich, but it gave both women a sense of fulfillment and they enjoyed the opportunity to meet with clients and business associates out of their houses.

Brenda had never followed her father's desires for her to go to law school. She figured that by marrying Jay, a lawyer, she had come close enough to checking that box.

After graduation she worked in her father's law office for six months, which she had found to be exceedingly boring. That cured her of the idea of going to law school. A couple of her college friends were sharing an apartment in Manhattan and invited her to join them. She found a job in the promotions department for a book publishing company. Brenda spent nine years there working her way up to assistant department director.

Along the way she met Jay. They married, lived in the city for a couple years before having Eric. They stayed in their small one-bedroom apartment for two more years before Steven was born. Then the walls had begun to close in on them.

Like other young couples they were looking for a place where they could raise their growing family. They wanted a dog. They wanted a yard. They wanted better public schools. New Jersey beckoned across the river.

After a couple years of childcare and commuting into the city, she became a stay-at-home Mom. By that time, Jay was a partner in his firm. He was making more than enough for them to live comfortably.

At first, she tried to freelance from home for her former company and some other publishers who she had met along the way. That plan died quickly when she discovered it was almost impossible to plan business calls and meetings around the demands of two highly active boys with complicated schedules.

She was now in the next phase of her life. The boys were both in high school and Jay had made senior partner. She and Debbie talked on the phone every day about their growing business. Once a month they got together for lunch to go over their financials and growth plans.

Business had brought them together, but they also had become friends. The previous year Debbie had shared with Brenda her dissatisfaction with her marriage and thoughts about getting a divorce. Brenda had consoled her and suggested that Debbie seek professional counseling. Debbie had done that and so far, was still married, although Brenda felt that a teapot was simmering in that relationship.

Ever since she had discovered that John Briggs had survived the war, Brenda had a growing desire to see him, talk to him, touch him, to know more about his life. She had not discussed this with anyone. Now she needed some advice, so it was Debbie's turn to help Brenda.

"I need to bounce something off you," Brenda said. Debbie assumed it was business related and got ready to take notes. "You can put down your pen and pad. This is more of a personal situation."

She paused making sure she had Debbie's full attention. Debbie was the ultimate multi-tasker, who tended to tune in to conversations but not be fully engaged. She would be thinking about five other things. Brenda wanted to make sure Debbie was listening.

"I met this guy when I was a senior in college. He was a Marine. Our backgrounds didn't exactly mesh. But the relationship got serious anyway. I really thought I loved him. Then he went to Vietnam. We exchanged a few letters but eventually that stopped.

"I moved on. After a while, I thought of him occasionally. And then I stopped thinking about him entirely. I assumed he moved on as well.

"Three years ago, we took the boys to Washington, DC, over Thanksgiving break. Just a short family vacation to show them the sites.

"We visited The Vietnam Wall. I wasn't necessarily looking for him. I was just sort of surfing over the names when I saw his name. John F. Briggs."

"Oh. My god." There was no question that Brenda had Debbie's full attention now. "You must have freaked."

"It really hit me. The memories. Just wondering how he had died. What his life was like in Vietnam? Wondering if he had thought of me. He certainly didn't have enough time to find another girlfriend. Did he suffer and then die from wounds or was it quick?

"In the past three years, there probably hasn't been a day go by that I haven't thought about him."

"Do you know what happened to him? Did you tell Jay about him? What about the boys?"

Brenda paused. "Hold on. There's more to tell you. And no. Jay does not know about him not that it would matter. It's been 25 years. Jay had other girlfriends before me. In fact, he was engaged to another woman before he and I met.

"Anyways, as Paul Harvey would say, 'now for the rest of the story.' It turns out that he didn't die in Vietnam. In fact, he's alive."

"Holy shit," Debbie responded. "This is like a Hollywood movie."

"Clerical errors were made in the data base. There are at least fourteen names they have found on The Wall of men who did not die. I read an article about it in The Times a couple weeks ago. He was even interviewed. He's alive living back in his hometown. Battle Creek, Michigan."

"Wow. Kellogg's Corn Flakes," Debbie said wistfully.

"Yep. And Tony the Tiger. Johnny is the only person I've ever known from Battle Creek."

Brenda showed Debbie the tracing of Briggs' name that she had done at The Wall and kept in her purse the past three years.

"What are you going to do? Are you going to call him? It would be great to see him again. Right?"

Brenda took time to reply. "I'm not sure it would be a good idea."

"That's not the entire story, is it?"

"No. It's not. We didn't just break up. It was more of a long, slow death. I didn't handle his going to Vietnam very well. He volunteered to go. Can you believe that? I felt like our relationship meant nothing to him. I was really pissed."

For the first time that Brenda had known her, Debbie was speechless. The silence lasted about a minute though it seemed more like a week.

"I would love to see him again. But, I don't know how to make that happen. I can't just tell Jay I'm going to see an old boyfriend. And I don't know what Johnny's family situation is like. He's probably married, got kids. He doesn't want some old girlfriend from 25 years ago showing up on his doorstep. He would probably think I was going to tell him about a love child."

"Was there one," Debbie asked.

"No. I was just joking about that."

"Wow. You said you wanted to bounce something off me. No shit. I would call this more like a boulder landing on my head," Debbie said.

They both laughed despite the seriousness of the moment.

"Let the dust settle," Debbie said. "It's only been a couple of weeks since you found this out. Your emotions are running high. You need to let some time pass."

Brenda didn't disagree. She took several deep breaths getting control of herself and preventing the desire to start crying in the middle of the restaurant. She knew Debbie was right although it didn't solve her dilemma. They talked for a few more minutes before adjourning. They were no longer in the mood to discuss business.

CHAPTER 35

October 1991
Battle Creek, Michigan

Briggs finished packing his suitcase. He was driving to Detroit's Metro Airport, about 100 miles east, to catch a flight to Washington, DC.

"John let's check to make sure you have all your medications," Sandy said. They both had joked that John was like a traveling drug store, he had so many prescriptions. She always ran him through a checklist before every trip, not unlike a pilot's airplane pre-check. They had been married seventeen years. She knew him well.

He was scheduled to be a speaker at a symposium on the impact of herbicides in warfare. This was the latest of many conferences, hearings and courtroom appearances Briggs had made since he became involved a decade before with Vietnam Veterans Assistance International.

VVAI's unofficial slogan was "Sprayed and Betrayed."

Killing time on one of his flights he tried to count how many trips he had made to the capitol. He stopped counting at thirty-three and figured there were at least ten more he couldn't remember. He felt that this is what it would be like to serve in Congress.

Despite government stonewalling and bureaucratic shell games, progress had been made. For years, the Veterans Administration had denied any connection between exposure to Agent Orange and human illness. Compensation, as little as it was, had finally begun to flow to veterans and their families who were living with symptoms consistent with toxic exposure.

He became a recognized expert on the effects of Agent Orange and the other Rainbow Herbicides: Green, Blue, Purple, White and Pink, that were identified by the color of the stripe painted on fifty-five-gallon barrels.

Following in his parents' footsteps, Briggs first career was as an accountant for the Kellogg's Company headquartered in Battle Creek. It was a company town.

His bosses were supportive of his efforts in VVAI allowing him to take time for travel and a flexible work schedule. He had become such a noted speaker and professional witness that they eventually found him a position and a desk down the street at the W.K. Kellogg Foundation, one of the largest philanthropic organizations in the nation, dedicated to supporting causes for children and families. A priority was focusing on birth defects. This was a better fit for him.

When questioned as to how an accountant had become an expert in a scientific field, he would jokingly explain that "an expert is a guy from out of town."

He understood the veterans' problems because he and his family were victims. He did not need a PhD in Science or a medical degree to understand what was happening to them. They lived with it every day of their lives.

He had been poked, prodded, x-rayed, tested and examined by more doctors than he could count starting at the Battle Creek Veterans' Hospital where he spent a year as a patient recovering from his war wounds. The proximity of the medical center to his home was one reason he had never considered becoming a corporate ladder climber which required location transfers. He needed to stay close to his doctors and the treatment at the VA.

Soldiers and veterans have been cared for in Battle Creek since 1917 when Fort Custer was built just six miles from the city center. It has served as a training base for America's military through two world wars, the Korean Conflict, the Vietnam War and now the Gulf War. The VA

Hospital, a military airfield and a national cemetery are adjacent to the base.

During World War II the Battle Creek Sanitarium was converted into one of the world's largest military hospitals specializing in amputations and the development of prothesis. It closed after the Korean Conflict.

Briggs had never fully recovered from the wounds, physical and emotional, he suffered during the battle in the DMZ. Nor would he. He had learned to live with them. His more critical problems were dealing with the cancer and the debilitating skin rashes that were a result of his exposure to Agent Orange.

Despite occasional bouts with depression he forced himself to show a sunny disposition to his family, friends and co-workers. Only Sandy and his doctors knew how much he suffered.

After Sandy miscarried twice, their only child, Todd, now 14 years old, was born with spinal bifida. Birth deformities were one of the common symptoms of fathers who had been exposed to Agent Orange. No one knew how many generations it would take to disappear.

It was the guilt that he carried because of his son's life and Sandy's burden that caused him the most grief. Sandy never blamed him. He blamed himself.

Had they known what they now knew about the effects of exposure to herbicides, different decisions might have been made. It was several years after the war that doctors and scientists were able to connect the dots and agree that Vietnam veterans had been poisoned by their own government. They were casualties of friendly fire.

As many times as he had testified in front of committees and in courtrooms, he had never gotten comfortable with being the point person for the men, women and families who suffer from their exposure to Agent Orange. Thousands of veterans and their families relied on him, and others, who had taken up the cause, to seek medical cures for their illnesses and provide financial compensation so they could live their lives without relying on charity or public assistance.

Achieving justice for the many victims of toxic poisoning of the Vietnam War had become a passion and a second career for Briggs.

He intensively prepared for every appearance. His testimony and speeches were carefully crafted, and he had learned how to deliver his lines effectively with sincerity and the appropriate amount of emotion and occasional humor.

"Let's check your briefcase," Sandy said. "Make sure you have your speech and all your notes."

"Yep. Check. Check," he responded flipping through the papers.

"Don't forget the Magic Markers. Here take a couple extra." He used them constantly to edit and rewrite his speeches right up until the last moment.

Sandy had watched his briefcase grow larger over the years. Even though he could give every speech without looking at his notes and prepared text, it was still a source of comfort to have a copy in front of him.

Sandy often traveled with him acting as his administrative assistant, taking notes, making observations and providing feedback. Since she was not making this trip, she wanted to make sure that he had everything he needed. She wasn't going this time because Todd needed her.

"Are you going to the Memorial to see your name," she asked. It had been eight months since the reporter called asking for his reaction to hearing that his name was one of the mistakes on The Wall.

"Probably not. I don't remember what day it was that I died."

"Don't joke about that. It's not funny."

He had never visited The Wall. He felt it would be too depressing, seeing those names, particularly Hornsby, thinking: "why him, not me? Just because I ducked, and he didn't."

"You do what makes you feel best. Good luck. See you in a couple of days." They kissed and gave each other a long hug. She waited in the driveway until the car disappeared around the corner.

CHAPTER 36

October 1991
Hyatt Regency Hotel Capitol Hill
Washington, DC

Brenda and Debbie drove down from New Jersey the night before to check into the hotel. This was their first time attending the Annual Convention of the Small Business Advisory Council.

The Hyatt was a short five-minute walk down the hill from the Capitol, making it the preferred meeting place for business and government. Members of Congress and their staff were more willing to attend events there rather than traveling across town.

After meeting for a $25 continental breakfast in the hotel restaurant, they had split up the various concurrent educational sessions between them. Brenda focused on anything that had to do with finance and government relations. Debbie went to the marketing seminars.

Besides the educational sessions, they hoped to meet prospective clients during the group lunches and cocktail parties. They were both experienced networkers. They had a side bet with each other, loser buys lunch, as to who would come home with the most business cards.

Listening to the speakers and the follow up Q&A gave Brenda an opportunity to think about their business and how to grow it. When she was working with client deadlines, then having to switch hats later in the day to take care of her family, it left little time for business strategizing. This was invigorating. She filled several pages of her notebook with ideas. She was sure Debbie was doing the same.

They connected at the mid-morning break. Both women agreed that the trip was already worth the expense. "I got one idea that will pay for this trip ten times over," Debbie commented. Both women spent the remainder of the break networking with the other attendees.

The afternoon sessions were scheduled to adjourn by 4:30 p.m. Attendance was traditionally less robust than the morning as energy levels began to dip after lunch. About 4 p.m. Brenda felt herself becoming sleepy as one of the sessions dragged on. Even the speakers seemed to be working with less enthusiasm. Most people were now looking forward to the cocktail party.

Brenda decided to slip out. Before heading to her room for a quick nap, she stopped first at the SBAC's literature table making sure she didn't miss anything that would be useful.

The entire basement floor of the hotel consisted of adjoining meeting rooms. There were several other groups holding conferences at the same time. Each organization had their own easel signage announcing the group and the session topic.

Brenda looked up as the door from one of the rooms across the hall opened. A man left and quickly headed for the restrooms at the end of the corridor.

She had a brief view of the speaker standing at the podium. From a distance he looked familiar. It was the way he cocked his head. She heard him speak a few words before the door slowly swung closed. It had been many years, but she knew the voice. She knew the look.

Brenda stood motionless while she registered what she thought she had just seen and heard. She later figured it was at least two minutes before she walked over to the easel to read the name of the organization. Vietnam Veterans Assistance International.

There was a registration table outside the room. The young woman who was behind the desk was busy typing out name badges and putting them into plastic holders, a never-ending job for meeting planners.

Brenda caught her eye and asked if she could look at the conference program. Without speaking or even looking up from her typewriter, the woman handed her a copy from the pile next to her.

A room down the hall adjourned. A large group of people flipped open the double doors and streamed down the corridor, talking loudly in a hurry to get to the bar.

Brenda almost got knocked over as she stood in their path intently searching the program for the name she knew had to be there.

"3 – 4:30 p.m. – PANEL DISCUSSION – Agent Orange Product Liability Litigation Update.

"PANELISTS – Eileen W. Meyers, Moorhead, Barker & Kerrigan, LLC, Washington, DC; J. Gordon Kline, American Society of Chemical Manufacturers, Reston, VA; Lawrence M. Colburn, Committee on the Assessment of Wartime Exposure to Herbicides in Vietnam, New York.

"Moderator: John F. Briggs, Vietnam Veterans Assistance Int., Battle Creek, MI."

The man who had left previously for a pit stop brushed by her and reentered the room. Brenda followed him and took a seat at the back. There were about 100 people spread around on the rows of chairs. She noted they were listening intently. Many were taking notes.

Briggs was conducting a Q & A between the panelists and the audience. Even though she wasn't listening to the discussion she noticed how skillfully he moderated the discussion. Her eyes were focused on him. She noticed that his left arm never moved. It just hung from his body. He favored his right side. The way he stood, resembled U.S. Senator Bob Dole who had lost use of one of his arms in World War II.

After fifteen minutes Briggs wrapped up the session.

"If there are no more questions, we will adjourn for the day. I'm sure the panelists will be glad to stick around for a few minutes if you want to talk to them individually. Let's give one last round of applause to our speakers and we'll see you at the reception that starts in," he paused looking at his watch, "about 45 minutes in the Governor's Room on the third floor."

Brenda stayed seated as the attendees picked up their bags and briefcases, chatting with each other, and filed from the room. Briggs packed up his papers, shared a handshake with one of the panelists and headed for the door.

She stood as he approached her. She noticed that he walked with a limp. His face was thin. His hair had turned gray. She noticed a scar that ran from his left ear along his jawline.

"Johnny."

"Yes?" He was used to people stopping him to ask questions about the session or offer additional comments. He wasn't used to people calling him "Johnny." He met her with a smile and a questionable look.

"Johnny. I'm Brenda. Brenda Kiley." It had been so long since she had used her maiden name, she almost felt like she was introducing someone else.

He didn't speak. He just looked at her. She thought maybe he didn't know her. Then she saw his eyes moisten. He started to reach for her as if he were going to hug her and then stopped.

"Oh my god," is all he could say.

It was an awkward moment. She needed to break the ice.

"Oh, c'mon. Give me a hug," she said as she reached out for him. "It's so great to see you."

The hug lasted just a few seconds. They stepped back from each other and then hugged a second time. This time they held on longer. Finally, they sat down as they both tried to figure out what to do or say next. The room had emptied.

"What are you doing here? Why are you here? Where do you live? Who are you now?" They both laughed as he realized he was just babbling.

"In order of your questions, I'm attending a business conference across the hall. The door to your session opened and I saw you at the podium. I live in New Jersey. And I'm the same person I was 25 years ago but now I'm married with two teenaged boys. My name now is Brenda Walker."

"I think I could use a drink," he said with a laugh.

"I agree. Maybe more than one. We have a lot of catching up to do."

Groups of noisy conventioneers were gathering in the lobby lounge, but Brenda and John found a corner table to themselves.

"I was here three years ago with my family. We visited The Wall. I saw your name. It hit me so hard. I thought about you often, wondering what you went through. How you died.

"Then I saw the article about the mistakes on The Wall. You were interviewed."

"Yeah. How about that? I became famous because I didn't die. I never quite found the time to get over there and see my name."

"You don't have to. I made a tracing of it. I've kept it in my purse for the past three years." She showed it to him.

"Ah. A picture of my gravestone." They both fell silent as he continued to look at it. She saw him tighten his lips and drop his head for a moment thinking he was going to continue talking. He didn't.

Brenda waited until the silence had become awkward.

"Tell me about yourself," she said.

"I guess I've grown up a lot since we last saw each other. I always felt that you were the adult in our relationship." They both laughed.

"First, I got blown up. That's why I walk the way I do. There is a lot of metal in my hip and upper leg. Shattered ear drums, this scar that took over 30 stitches, and more shrapnel wounds than you can count. Some of it is still in there.

"When they took me off the hill, they rang me up as being dead. That's how my name got on The Wall. They were getting ready to put me in a body bag and ship me home when some Navy nurse saw me twitch. I lived but someone forgot to change the records."

They shared the basics about their lives and families. John told her about Sandy and Todd, skipping over the details other than to say that his son had some health issues. He told her about his job at Kellogg's and his passion, being an advocate for victims of Agent Orange.

He described the problems that the victims suffered without mentioning his own cancer.

"Do you remember Brandon Hayes? He was the Army officer that was dating your friend when we went to the formal. He was my comrade in arms when I punched out that drunk frat boy."

"Yeah. I do. He was going to be a helicopter pilot, wasn't he?"

"That's the one. I met him through the VVAI. His story is not a pretty one. He flew a lot of missions spreading Agent Orange. He died of cancer about a year ago.

"He testified at one of our hearings about how he would go out to the flight line in the morning and they would have the cannisters hooked up to his helicopter. He didn't know that it would poison him. Besides, what could he do? An order was an order. There was no saying 'no.' They would open the chutes and if the wind were blowing the wrong way the mist would fill the cockpit. We've had several chopper pilots die of cancer."

He asked about Brenda and her family. She downplayed her life story. She gave him an update on her parents and brother. She recognized that she had experienced little adversity in her life when compared to his.

She had a husband she loved who had a successful career. They had two great kids, plenty of money with a beautiful house in an upscale neighborhood. The worst thing she could think of in her life was when she broke her arm once when she fell while playing tennis. Their lives had gone in such different directions.

They talked about their times together back in Virginia. "Do you remember that bar we used to go to?" John asked. "Goldy's. That was the name Right? Goldy was a real character if my memory is correct. We had some fun times there." She nodded in agreement.

"Johnny. Why did you leave? Why did you go to Vietnam when you didn't have to go?"

Other than his mother, Brenda was the only one to call him Johnny. Sandy never called him by that name. He had outgrown it by the time they met. To everyone else he was John or Briggsy. Johnny was just for his mother and the first lover in his life. He smiled, took a sip of his drink, leaned back and took a deep breath.

"It wasn't the best decision I ever made. That's for sure. It changed my life. It changed Sandy's and Todd's. Maybe it changed yours too.

"Although, it appears to me that you've done well. I'm happy for you."

"Thank you," she replied.

"I've thought about it so many times. Laying in a VA hospital you have lots of time to think about your life. I have wondered where you were and what your life was like. Sandy and I have a good marriage, but first love is a sweet memory. It has never left me.

"A lot of guys went to Vietnam spouting the Marine Corps rah rah gung-ho bullshit. That wasn't me. It is hard to explain to anyone, myself included. It all sounds empty now. Courage or sheer stupidity? It was like a magnet pulling me there.

"I guess I felt an obligation to go, be part of something important that was happening in the world. I had read that you only discover what you are made of in times of war. I believed it.

"I wanted to know how I would react in combat. Turned out I did okay. I never fired my rifle. Not once in ten months. But, when we got hit the night I was wounded, I did what I was trained to do. I didn't flinch. I didn't let anybody down. I was scared but I wasn't a coward."

"Does that mean anything to you now?" Brenda asked.

"Yes. It does. I know you don't understand it. Most people don't. After living with me for years Sandy sort of gets it, or at least she tells me she does. We don't talk about it. It does mean something to me. A few of my old Marine buddies who I stay in touch with, they understand it."

"So maybe it is some Marine Corps rah-rah gung-ho bullshit but by another name," Brenda said.

"I can't argue with you on that. People who join the Marines are a different personality type. We need to test ourselves. It doesn't make a lot of sense when you're 47 years old. But it does when you're 22."

They sat in silence each dealing with their own thoughts.

"The obligation I felt was to younger Marines. I was the old man at 22. Most of the Marines fighting the war were 18, 19, 20 years old. I was expected to help them survive."

"Did you?"

"I like to think that I did. I paid a price for that decision. I should say we have paid a price. My family did too. I went to Vietnam accepting the fact that I could be wounded or killed. I did not think I would be poisoned by my own guys. A poison that I passed on to my wife and son."

Briggs told Brenda about Sandy's miscarriages and Todd's spinal bifida and his own cancer. He had just completed a round of chemotherapy two weeks before. He did not expect his condition to get any better.

"It would be easy to be bitter, but I refuse to let that happen. It doesn't do any good. I made that decision to go to Vietnam based on the information I had at the time. It was what I knew and what I believed. It doesn't do any good to dwell on it.

"I've done my best to turn a negative into a positive working for Agent Orange victims, here in the U.S. and in Vietnam. That became my passion."

She sat quietly as he told her about his work with the VVAI. He told her about the lawsuits won and lost. He summarized the cancers, the birth defects, the emotional toll and the environmental destruction of Vietnam.

"I never had any idea about all this Johnny. I guess I am embarrassed to say that once the war was over, I put it out of my mind, at least until the day I saw your name on The Wall. I'm so proud of you and what you are doing."

They ran out of time. Brenda said she needed to meet up with Debbie. John had a meeting with the VVAI Board of Directors, then he was flying home in the morning.

They walked out of the lounge together and stopped in the lobby to say goodbye. They hugged neither one wanting to let go. She did not want him to see her tears. He did not want her to see his tears.

"Johnny, it was so great to see you. I am so happy that was a mistake on The Wall. You lived. I want you to know that I loved you and I will always be thinking of you."

"Brenda, the only mistake on that wall was that they got the date wrong. I was killed in Vietnam. I just haven't died yet."

* * * * * * * * * *

Vietnam War Timeline: There were 57,939 names inscribed on The Wall at its dedication in 1982. The last name was on Panel W1, Line 132. U.S. Air Force Second Lieutenant Richard Vandegeer, 27, Columbus, Ohio, a helicopter pilot, died May 15, 1975. So far, 32 mistakes have been identified on The Wall.

The Author

James Elsener spent his early years in southern Michigan. After one unsatisfactory year of college he enlisted in the United States Marine Corps. He served as a radio operator with an artillery unit in Vietnam.

After 47 years he retired from the newspaper industry during which he was a reporter, columnist, editor, publisher and sales manager.

He now splits his time between Chicago and Michigan. *"Reflections of Valour"* is his second novel. *"The Last Road Trip"* was published in 2018 and is available on Amazon in print and e-book formats.

Contact the author at jimelsener@hotmail.com.

References

Vietnam War Almanac, James H. Willbanks, 2010, Checkmark Books, New York, NY. ISBN 978-0-8160-7102-9

The Vietnam War: An Almanac. World Almanac Publishing. Harry G. Summers, Jr., Colonel of Infantry, Ballantine Books, NY, Copyright 1985 – ISBN 0-7394-4290-2

U.S. Marines in Vietnam – The Landing and the Build Up 1965, Jack Shulimson and Major Charles M. Johnson, USMC. History and Museums Division Headquarters, U.S. Marine Corps, Washington, D.C. 1978. Library of Congress Card No. 78-600120.

U.S. Marines in Vietnam – An Expanding War 1966, Jack Shulimson, History and Museums Division Headquarters, U.S. Marine Corps, Washington, D.C. 1982. Library of Congress Card No. 82-600567.

U.S. Marines in Vietnam – Fighting the North Vietnamese 1967, Major Gary L. Telfer, USMC, Lieutenant Colonel Lane Rogers, USMC and V. Keith Fleming, Jr.; History and Museums Division Headquarters, U.S. Marine Corps, Washington, D.C. 1984. Library of Congress Card No. 77-604776.

Fire for Effect – Artillery Forward Observers in Korea, Anthony J. Sobieski, 2005, Author House, ISBN: 1-4208-3836-9 (sc) ISBN: 98-1-4685-2597-7 (ebk).

Waiting for an Army to Die – The Tragedy of Agent Orange, Second Edition, Fred A. Wilcox, 2011. First Seven Stories Press. eISBN: 978-1-60980-339-1.

Scorched Earth – Legacies of Chemical Warfare in Vietnam, Fred A. Wilcox, 2011, Seven Stories Press First Edition. eISBN: 978-1-60980-340-7.

Acknowledgements

I spent eight months and 22 days in I Corps, South Vietnam, in 1966 serving in an artillery unit as a radio operator, just like John Briggs. I consider that to be my original research. I then let 54 years elapse before writing a book about what I saw, what I heard and what I experienced.

Your memory gets foggy after this amount of time. This is a work of fiction.

The characters are composites of people I knew. Descriptions of locations were as best as I could remember them. The combat scenes were how I imagined them to be.

I tried to capture the reality of the war that I experienced. I wanted to be accurate with military protocol, weapons, equipment, and strategies. I had to refresh my memories and understanding of the war's history.

To make sure I was accurate with my descriptions of military life, I first turned to the men who I served with a half century ago. I wanted to make sure I didn't disappoint them as I recaptured experiences, customs and terminology.

First Sergeant Donald Plavnick (USMC Retired) was a walking encyclopedia. He was always my first point of reference when I needed more information about all things military. Don was a unique presence in my life for 57 years. He died from the effects of Covid 19 just as I was finishing the final draft of the novel. Don, deservedly so, was buried in Arlington National Cemetery.

The first three people who read the initial draft are former Marines: John Russell, Bill Donohue and Mike Forhan. I served with each of them. I wanted to make sure I had it right before asking other people to read the manuscript. Thanks for your continuing friendship and your efforts to make this book as readable and accurate as possible.

My second group of Beta readers are all former journalists: my wife Pat Elsener who I met when we both worked at the Chicago Tribune. Pat made significant suggestions to the manuscript, character development and title. She is also my constant source of encouragement.

Thanks also to Richard Rotman, my colleague from my first journalism job at the City News Bureau of Chicago; and Mike Conklin, retired from a career at the Chicago Tribune. Both are published authors.

Others who read the early draft and gave important feedback were my Michigan friends Susan Neidlinger and Dennis Jewett and my brother George Elsener.

I borrowed the name for the main character in this novel from my friend John Briggs, a former Marine who I first met in 1964. The real "Briggsy" and I continue to share warm memories from those days of youthful friendship.

Colonel Bill Dow (US Army Retired), a former artillery officer who I met on a golf course on St. Simons Island, Georgia, helped me accurately describe an artillery fire mission and clarify the vocabulary.

Thanks go to Tim Tetz, Director of Outreach at the Vietnam Veterans Memorial Fund, who promptly answered all my phone calls and e-mails. His help was invaluable in providing accurate information about the "The Wall." At last count there were 32 names of men whose names were included by mistake.

In Chicago, where I live, we are blessed with a terrific resource, the Pritzker Military Museum and Library. I offer a salute to Leah Cohen and Teresa Embrey who so expertly guided me to the resources I needed to provide an overall understanding of the war.

MORE BY JAMES ELSENER

THE LAST ROAD TRIP

(AVAILABLE AT AMAZON.COM IN PAPERBACK AND KINDLE FORMATS)

Stub Rowe's mediocre major league baseball career ended with a ground out to the second baseman. He considered that to be the wimpiest out in baseball.

He had never been a star, but for a few years he was considered steady and reliable. Some team always needed a third baseman with a little pop in his bat...until the years ran out on him.

He hadn't given a lot of thought to retirement. Now it was staring him in the face as he considered what marketable skills he possessed.

His ex-wife and children seemed to be getting along fine without him. He had a few high maintenance personal relationships with *"baseball annies"* that needed repair and closure.

So, he decided to take a drive across the country that he had mostly seen from 30,000 feet. He wanted to see sights that he missed when he was traveling from city to city to play baseball.

He would visit former teammates and old friends along the way but discovered that the passage of years had changed relationships.

Then he had to step up for an emergency. His sister's family was in trouble, and he was the only one that could help them out. He wasn't used to taking responsibility for other people. Meanwhile, the financial nest egg that he had built was dwindling away at a much faster rate than expected.

Finding a job in the real world when you haven't had one in 20 years proved to be a challenge. Being a baseball lifer was his other option. Hopefully, this trip would give him the chance to find a fit in life and a path forward.

It's a novel with a message told with humor, irony and human experience.

CPSIA information can be obtained
at www.ICGtesting.com
Printed in the USA
LVHW050727181121
703571LV00017B/839